In Reverence and Awe

The Practice of Leading Worship with Excellence

Enoch Liao

Copyright © 2019 by **Enoch Liao**

All rights reserved. No part of this publication may be reproduced, distributed, or transmitted in any form or by any means, without prior written permission.

Unless otherwise specified, all Scripture quotations are taken from The ESV® Bible (The Holy Bible, English Standard Version®) copyright © 2001 by Crossway, a publishing ministry of Good News Publishers. ESV® Text Edition: 2011. The ESV® text has been reproduced in cooperation with and by permission of Good News Publishers. Unauthorized reproduction of this publication is prohibited. Used by permission. All rights reserved.

Scripture quotations marked (NASB) are taken from the New American Standard Bible ® (NASB), copyright © 1960, 1962, 1963, 1968, 1971, 1972, 1973, 1975, 1977, 1995 by The Lockman Foundation. Used by permission. www.Lockman.org.

Scripture quotations marked (NIV) ® are taken from the Holy Bible, New International Version ®. Copyright © 1973, 1978, 1984, 2011 by Biblica, Inc.® Used by permission. All rights reserved worldwide.

Scripture quotations marked (NKJV) are taken from the New King James Version®. Copyright © 1982 by Thomas Nelson, Inc. Used by permission. All rights reserved.

Renown Publishing

In Reverence and Awe / Enoch Liao
ISBN-13: 978-1-952602-19-1

To all who would lead others to the One who alone is worthy of all worship.

CONTENTS

A Note from the Author 5
The Fire That Fuels Worship 9
Part One: Team 15
Chapter One: Not Just a "Music Team" 17
Chapter Two: The Most Important Instrument 23
Chapter Three: Artists or Leaders? 33
Chapter Four: Competency or Character? 47
Chapter Five: Best Practices for Better Songs 61
Chapter Six: Raising Teams 75
Chapter Seven: My Experience in Building Worship Teams
.... 87
Part Two: Pick the Best Songs 99
Chapter Eight: The Song's Message 101
Chapter Nine: The Song's Music— Honor Through Excellence 113
Chapter Ten: The Song's Match— Fit the Context 121
Part Three: Sets 133
Chapter Eleven: Start with a Theme, Mood, or Song 135
Chapter Twelve: Think Movements, Not Songs 145
Chapter Thirteen: Set Flow— Planning the Dynamics 155
Chapter Fourteen: Two Kinds of Songs— Focusing and Expressing 169
Chapter Fifteen: Creating Balance in a Single Set 183
Chapter Sixteen: Creating Balance for Multiple Sets 193
Chapter Seventeen: End Worship with a Bang! 203

Part Four: Leading 209
Chapter Eighteen: The True Worship Leader 211
Chapter Nineteen: Orderliness and Expressiveness in Worship 219
Chapter Twenty: Good Repute Takes Time 227
Chapter Twenty-One: No Mini-Sermons Needed 235
Chapter Twenty-Two: Worship with Scripture 243
Chapter Twenty-Three: Solo Performances and Interludes 251
Chapter Twenty-Four: Memorize Your Sets 261
Chapter Twenty-Five: Introducing an Unfamiliar Song 273
Chapter Twenty-Six: Worship Cues for the Band 281
Chapter Twenty-Seven: Eyes—Open or Closed? 293
Chapter Twenty-Eight: When Things Don't Go As Planned 301
Chapter Twenty-Nine: Ask—Did Worship Go Well? 311
Chapter Thirty: Pastors Versus Worship Leaders 317

Part Five: Notes 323
Chapter Thirty-One: Sample Letters for Church Leaders. 325
Chapter Thirty-Two: A Note for the Pastor 331
Chapter Thirty-Three: A Note for the Slide Operator 341
Chapter Thirty-Four: A Note for the Sound Person 351
Chapter Thirty-Five: A Note for the Vocalist 357
Chapter Thirty-Six: A Note for the Drummer, Percussionist, and Bassist 367
Chapter Thirty-Seven: A Note for the Guitarist 379
Chapter Thirty-Eight: A Note for the Band Leader 389
Chapter Thirty-Nine: A Note for the Worship Team 397
It Starts with You 405
Notes 407

Song Categorizing Worksheet 409
Set Assessment Checklist 411
Samples of "Call to Worship" 413
About the Author 425

PREFACE

A Note from the Author

I originally wrote this book for the handful of worship leaders in my life who happen to have a strange and curious interest in what I think about the topic. I suppose that's natural, as I am a teaching pastor in my humble church. So, if you're a part of the church in which I serve, then here you go. Here's what I think and care about pertaining to worship leading. I've since revised this project because more people outside of my church began to ask me for copies.

I've been leading worship and planning worship sets for about twenty years. This does not make me an expert, however. Far from it! But I have learned a few things about what *not* to do when planning a worship set. I've also discovered the principles I use for assembling a worship set that seem to be effective in leading people to worship God.

Not only am I *not* an expert worship leader, I am not an expert musician. But perhaps that helps me write for my intended audience of local church worship leaders. Most of them are not professional musicians either.

I wrote this book for Christians who desire to serve as worship leaders or "lead-worshipers." The type of worship leading I'm talking about is leading a Christian congregation in the corporate, musical worship of God.

Most of what I share in this book are lessons I learned after stepping out of my role as a weekly worship leader, when I was able to participate in the pew like everyone else. I originally shared my thoughts with a few people who I thought might be receptive to my ideas. To my surprise, others showed interest in my thoughts. So, I decided to put these ideas down on paper.

I wrote a seven-page document entitled "How I Put Together a Worship Set" back in 2005. Surprisingly, that little paper found its way to more people and more churches than I anticipated, to about three churches and fifteen individuals!

Since people seemed to want more, and I had more to say, I decided to sit down and expand on those ideas. It turned out I had a lot to say!

During a sabbatical in 2011, I spent several weeks expanding those seven pages into the project you now hold in your hands. And even after writing all this, I have more on my heart to share with others. But for now, this project will have to suffice.

I realize that most of these ideas are not explicit in the Bible. I think, however, they fit with biblical doctrines. This is similar to preaching methods. Very few actual preaching methods can be drawn from Scripture, yet we teach them with conviction because they seem to fit with what Scripture does tell us about preaching. There's no Bible text on what makes a good introduction, how to grab attention, or how to deliver a sermon, but there are many good examples. So, while I believe in the principles in this book, I'm glad to admit these may not apply to everybody the way Scripture should.

In these pages, you'll find the principles I use to plan a worship set, whether it be for a ten-person small group or a worship service with several hundred participants. I've never led worship for thousands at a time, so I can't say from experience how these play out in those situations. But I don't see why they would change once you move past, say, the seven-hundred mark.

I mention numerous worship songs throughout the book. Most evangelical Christians will recognize these songs, but not all. I hope you can grasp my points without recognizing all the songs I use as examples.

This book consists of five parts, and there is a logic and reason behind its structure. I believe that the worship ministry of a local church begins not with the music or technical aspects of leading congregational singing, but with the consideration of the individuals who will make up the worship team.

After considering people for worship ministry, I then move into technical aspects of this craft. First, I consider individual songs, and what worship leaders should take into account when selecting songs. Next, I discuss how to combine those songs to form worship sets. Third, I deal with practical issues of leading congregational singing.

You may find the final part of the book useful to give to particular individuals in your church or ministry, such as the pastor, the sound engineer, the various instrumentalists, and so forth. These chapters deal with particular aspects of each of the aforementioned roles, as I have observed in worship ministry. Consider giving the appropriate chapter to that particular person and allow me to advocate for you or explain a perspective for you that may come across better from someone else.

At the end of each chapter of this book, workbook sections are provided to help you search your own heart and commit to a lifestyle of worship.

Finally, I want to offer some thanks.

Thanks to my church, Boston Chinese Evangelical Church, for granting me a sabbatical during which I could write the first draft of this project.

Thanks to all the worship teams and worship leaders for sharing their experiences and struggles with me.

Thanks to my family for letting me get away to Starbucks, Panera Bread, or Kung Fu Tea to write this.

Thanks to God for being worthy of all our worship.

INTRODUCTION

The Fire That Fuels Worship

> *Therefore let us be grateful for receiving a kingdom that cannot be shaken, and thus let us offer to God acceptable worship, with reverence and awe, for our God is a consuming fire.*
> **—Hebrews 12:28–29**

Christians in America often associate the term *worship* with music or a Sunday worship service. So many who write about worship point out that worship should go beyond music and Sundays. I agree. But I want to take it further than medium and mode. I want to take it to new places.

The Trinitarian God—Father, Son, and Holy Spirit—of Christianity is the Almighty over an unshakable kingdom. This God has offered that very kingdom to sinful humanity. God secured that offer by paying for humanity's sins through the sacrifice of His Son (John 3:16). God sustains that offer through the down payment of His Spirit (Ephesians 1:13–14). The kingdom is worth a King's ransom. That ransom was paid by King Jesus Himself when He died on the cross.

Scripture calls us to be grateful for receiving this

kingdom that cannot be shaken. "And thus," the writer of Hebrews concludes, "we should offer to God acceptable worship."

What is this acceptable worship? Worship with an attitude of reverence and awe.

Reverence means to deeply respect something. And awe is a mixture of fear and wonder. It's the feeling I get when I look at fire, whether on a candle or in a firepit. The flame moves in ways I can't predict. It interests me. I am drawn to it. I could watch fire for hours, and I have.

The funny thing about fire is this: I think I control it, but I really don't. Yes, I can choose to blow it out, if it's on a birthday candle. But that's not controlling fire; that's extinguishing it. I merely choose to consume the fire before it consumes me. The moment I forget to respect fire is the moment fire can overwhelm me.

In light of this discussion about fire, let us recall that Scripture calls God a "consuming fire." We should offer God acceptable worship with reverence and awe because our God is a consuming fire. When we forget that God is the Almighty Creator with a wrath as fierce as His mercy is wide, that's the moment His fire can consume us.

God is not like the tiny flame on a birthday candle. God is not like fire contained in a fireplace. God is not like fire on a cooking grill. God is an all-consuming fire—the kind that is capable of consuming city blocks or forest acres. The great aid for our worship comes by respecting God with a mixture of fear and wonder.

It might seem that writing a book about worshiping this awesome, consuming God is an insurmountable task. But it is necessary. Not necessary that I, myself, write a book, but that *someone* does.

What is my qualification to write? I boast of no greater qualification than anyone else who has touched flame and felt its burn, and then looked at that fire with a newfound respect and fear, reverence and awe.

WORKBOOK

Introduction Questions

Question: Based on Scripture, write your personal definition of worship. What should the attitude of a worshipper be?

_____
_____
_____
_____
_____
_____
_____
_____
_____
_____
_____
_____

Question: What is the relationship of music to worship?

_____
_____
_____
_____
_____
_____
_____
_____
_____
_____
_____

Introduction Notes

Part One:
Team

PART ONE: TEAM

Chapter One:
Not Just a "Music Team"

Before you try to form a worship team, consider the kind of team you want to build. Many Christian groups have a "music team." The music team leads the singing at events like Sunday worship services. This descriptor fails, however, to capture the team's purpose. "Music team" describes the medium, but it says little about the mission.

Train your teams to think of themselves not as *music* teams but as *worship* teams. What's the difference? A music team leads music. But a worship team leads worship. Consider this:

- Music teams lead people in singing. Worship teams lead people in worship.

- Music teams stop leading when the music stops. Worship teams continue to direct people to worship God all the time.

- Music teams gather for the common mission of making wonderful music—a good cause. Worship teams gather for the common mission to worship a wonderful Maker—the highest cause.

- Music teams want people to hear great music. Worship teams want people to hear from a great God.

Worship teams, in this context, must all be music teams. But not all music teams are worship teams. A team could be a great music team but a lousy worship team. Music teams can do just fine while living in hypocrisy and sin. Worship teams cannot lead with unrepentant sin.

- Music teams can play superb music while jealous or angry with one another. Worship teams cannot honor God while unreconciled to one another (Matthew 5:21–24).
- Music teams succeed when people say, "I love your sound!" Worship teams succeed when people say, "I love your God!"

We don't need to be legalistic about terms. You don't need to correct every person who says, "music team" instead of "worship team." But those in Christian leadership must hold the mission clearly in our minds.

We define a *worship team* as a team whose passion and mission is to direct people to the glory and praise of God, mainly through musical, corporate worship.

So, how can you tell if your teams are serving like music teams or worship teams? Ask this question: Do we pray for our ministry?

Our prayer requests reveal our focus. What do we pray for? Do we pray for a great sound? Do we pray that all the members practice and perform properly? Do we pray that God provide a drummer or a bass guitarist? These prayers are fine, but they are about music.

Let us not just pray for great music; we must also pray for true worship. We should pray for hearts of worship. We should pray that our team members grow in love and obedience to Christ. We should pray that the Holy Spirit move our hearts to worship. We should pray that the congregation respond to God through lives of hope and obedience.

You don't have to be Christian to make great music. We have plenty of examples of fantastic musicians who don't profess Christ. You don't have to be Christian to move people with music. But leading worship is not about moving people with music. It's about moving people to worship, and that is a supernatural transaction. Human effort alone cannot move people to worship in Spirit and in truth (John 4:24). Only God can do that. Thus, the Holy Spirit is the true worship leader.

Evaluate your team's mind-set. Are you a music team trying to make great music? Or are you a worship team trying to make much of our great God?

WORKBOOK

Chapter One Questions

Your Heart: Based on the descriptions given, would you say that you have been leading worship or leading music? What is the evidence that corroborates your answer? What about others on your team?

_____

_____

_____

_____

_____

_____

_____

_____

_____

_____

Your Church: Is your church responsive to music or worship? Does the congregation respond more to a talented performance or to revelation of the character and person of God? How can you tell?

_____
_____
_____
_____
_____
_____
_____
_____
_____
_____

Your Commitment: Write out a prayer list that will help your team focus on "worship" over "music." How will you pray for yourself, your team, and your congregation?

_____
_____
_____
_____
_____

Chapter One Notes

PART ONE: TEAM

Chapter Two:
The Most Important Instrument

> *I appeal to you therefore, brothers, by the mercies of God, to present your bodies as a living sacrifice, holy and acceptable to God, which is your spiritual worship. Do not be conformed to this world, but be transformed by the renewal of your mind, that by testing you may discern what is the will of God, what is good and acceptable and perfect.*
> *—Romans 12:1-2*

Many pastors and leaders have already written helpful books on worship using Romans 12, so I didn't plan to address that topic. However, Romans 12:1-2 comes up again and again in worship articles for a very good reason: It's one of the best biblical texts about worship as a lifestyle.

It may sound trite, but it's true. The most important worship instrument is you. It's not the singing voice or the organ or the guitar or the piano or even the shaker. I know this may be hard to believe.

Worship leaders must understand the difference between loving God and loving *to worship* God. It's easy to confuse loving God with loving to sing songs about God.

Many people, including non-Christians, delight in singing about God. For that matter, many people love to sing, regardless of what the song lyrics say. In fact, entire musical genres have songs about Jesus or the Christian life. Think of genres like African American spirituals, or gospel music, or some American country music.

But many who sing or perform those songs may not love God. Some may not even believe in God. Thus, worship leaders must reflect upon *why* people sing (or don't sing) during congregational worship. Do they sing because they love God, or because they love singing?

To truly love God means to glorify Him not just in song, but with one's whole life. That's because worship is not mainly about making beautiful music. It's about making beautiful lives that please and honor God.

The Bible compares a beautiful life in Christ to a *fragrant aroma* (2 Corinthians 2:15–16). Worshiping God with our lives entails living in such a way that God "*through us* spreads the knowledge of him everywhere" (emphasis added). Thus, worship does not just take place when we are at church or singing worship songs. Worshiping God is something that happens all the time and everywhere. If you're a worship leader in a Christian church, you've probably already heard this. Ah, but do you do this?

Whole Life Worship

Worship is more than just singing, as we see in Romans 12. Worship is about how we treat our neighbors, our families, and even those who try to cause trouble in our lives. I use the term "Whole-Life Worship" to describe using every aspect of our life to worship our Lord. I want to address three areas of life where I see most people struggle to incorporate whole-life worship: in our neighborhoods, in our families, and in our pews.

Lead Worship with Your Neighbors

If worship leading is pointing people to a great God, then leading worship with one's neighbors means pointing one's neighbors to God. This does not require us to invite our neighbors to a service in our home to sing worship songs, though that could be part of it. What this means is that our lives of worship help point people to the God we worship and live for.

And by "neighbor," I don't mean to confine worship leading to those who physically live next door to you. That's not how Jesus used the term "neighbor" in His parable about the Good Samaritan (Luke 10:25–37). In that passage, a neighbor was anyone you meet, whether in your apartment building, down the street, or in your travels abroad. This includes those you encounter in daily life: people living next door, people who pick up your trash, people who pump your gas, people who do your taxes.

Jesus said, "Let your light so shine before men, that they may see your good works and glorify your Father in heaven" (Matthew 5:16 NKJV).

If your church saw your interactions with others, would they still follow your example in worship? Do you show grace to your neighbors? Are you kind and gracious to those who serve you? Do you seek to care for the poor around you? Do you concern yourself with the injustices in our cities and world? Do you show the fruit of the Spirit by the way you drive? You should. You should lead worship all the time.

Lead Worship for Your Family

Second, lead worship for your family. If you lead worship for the church family, you should lead worship for your own family. If you direct congregants to God, you should also direct your spouse, children, or housemates to

God.

Your family members and housemates see a different side of you than most people. They see how you are at home, how you use your time, and how you treat others. Often, those in our household have a more accurate picture of who we really are. So, how do those in your home respect you as a worship leader?

Is our worship leading outside the home consistent with our worship leading in the home? Most worship leaders understand they are called to lead their congregations by example. How much more should a worship leader lead by example in the home?

To lead worship for your family, you also should graciously yet honestly consider your family's spiritual wellbeing. If your family has members who are not worshiping the Lord with their lives, then you must evaluate and pray to address any problems. Of course, no family is perfect, and we need not be legalistic. But if a family member, such as a spouse or a child, appears to live in a direction that will take them further from Jesus, then you must consider your priorities. Talk to a trusted and compassionate pastor or fellow leader. Share your concerns for your family with them.

This issue is not so much about maintaining a good reputation as a worship leader—though that is important. This issue is about priorities. What's the value in pointing others to God if those we love the most need us to point them to God? Perhaps this is God's way of directing you to where you are most needed. Other people can be worship leaders for the congregation. But no one else can be a dad, mom, sibling, or child for your family.

Lead Worship from the Pew

There are times when you won't be on the platform in the front of the congregation. You're still a worship leader on those days. People may recognize you when you sit among the congregation. They may whisper to each other, "Hey, that's the worship leader from last week." They are still watching you.

They'll notice if you're distracted during worship. They'll observe your expressiveness in singing. They'll notice if you don't "get into" the worship as much as you urge others to get into it when you lead. They'll notice if you don't lift your hands during a song that you urged the congregation to lift their hands. They'll notice if you look at your cell phone or read your program during a time of prayer.

Or, they will notice if you lead well from the pew. They'll notice you sing along even if the band is off. They'll notice if you lift your hands even if the song leader didn't ask. They'll notice if you arrive on time for church (especially if the week before you scolded people for being late!).

In short, they'll notice how your worship in the pew compares or contrasts with your worship on the stage.

Whatever they notice, they will remember the next time you step up on the platform. If they saw you in the pew distracted, disengaged, and disconnected from the worship, they will lose respect for you. If they saw you in the pew engaged, attentive, and expressive, your leadership gains respect and credibility. Lead worship from the pew, even when you're following—*especially* when you're following.

Too many worship leaders forget that people will follow their worship leader even in the absence of a musical instrument, microphone, or hymnal. So, lead worship at all times.

WORKBOOK

Chapter Two Questions

Your Heart: Do you love worshiping God (i.e. singing, presenting music) or do you love God Himself? In what other ways are you actively engaging in "whole life worship," particularly in your community? Are there areas of your life that negate the worship message you present to the church?

_____
_____
_____
_____
_____
_____
_____
_____
_____

Your Church: Notice the attitude of those in the pews during worship. Are people focused on and participating in worship, or are they distracted and disconnected? How can you and your team model "worship from the pew"? Are there worshippers that you could place strategically throughout the congregation to model worshipful attitudes that will encourage others to focus on God?

_____

_____

_____

_____

_____

_____

_____

_____

_____

_____

_____

Your Commitment: Evaluate and/or recommit yourself to a time of "family worship," (connecting with God together) whether that is devotions and prayer with your spouse, a Bible story and song with your children, or an in-depth book study with a roommate. How will you model "whole life worship" with your family as you go about errands, chores, and leisure time together?

Chapter Two Notes

PART ONE: TEAM

Chapter Three:
Artists or Leaders?

Why does it seem like we have only one or the other? One church is stuck with godly leaders who just don't cut it musically. Another church has plenty of gifted musicians, but they are not spiritually ready to lead anyone in worship.

Musical talent or spiritual maturity? Perhaps within your smaller church you've faced this very choice when considering potential worship team members.

One potential worship leader has a great heart to serve. She is teachable and welcomes feedback. She shows up faithfully to practices on time. But musically she's off some of the time. Okay, maybe she's musically off much of time. But her heart is the right place.

Another potential worship leader is a young and gifted musician. He plays multiple instruments well. Others in your church appreciate how much his talents add to the musical aspect of the worship. But he's not reliable and doesn't take criticism well.

How do we deal with this dilemma of seeming to be forced to choose between musical talent or spiritual maturity? The good news is that we don't have to settle for just one or the other. God invites us and enables us to develop people in both musical competency and personal character. The key is to develop each trait accordingly.

Artistic Leaders and Leading Musicians

Musical worship leaders serve two roles. First, they serve as artists—they are musicians who are generally passionate about their craft. Second, they serve as spiritual leaders leading people to worship God. However, most worship leaders identify more with one of these roles than both. They either consider themselves musicians who lead worship, or they see themselves as leaders who play music.

These roles often cause tension. Artists and leaders want different things. Artists desire beauty, expression, and technical excellence. On the other hand, leaders desire to rally people toward some goal and marshal the resources to achieve that goal.

Artists express themselves and seek an audience. Leaders seek followers to express their leadership. Artists do art. Leaders lead.

It's hard enough to excel as either a leader or an artist, let alone both. Artists and leaders tend to possess different strengths and weaknesses. An effective worship leader who excels both in art and leadership is the exception.

In my experience, a worship leader usually starts out as a musician or as a leader. Whatever role he starts with, he develops experience in the other role as he serves on a worship team. Thus, there are leaders who become musicians and musicians who become leaders.

Why does this matter? It matters because worship leaders need qualities of both the musician and the leader to effectively lead worship. And it matters because artists and leaders develop differently. Both you and the worship leader will get frustrated if you try to train an artist the way you would train a leader, and vice versa. Artists and leaders have different pathways to growth. We need wisdom to train leaders to be artists and artists to be leaders. Let's consider each pathway in turn.

The Leader-Turned-Musician

First, the leader-turned-musician sees himself as a leader who plays music. This person usually started leading worship out of a need in the community. This leader stepped forward to help out. This leader volunteered to fill a void in the music ministry. First and foremost, this person saw a need and met it as best he could. This person had a heart for worship and knew the importance of cultivating worship in the church. That the need was music-related was secondary. The leader would use whatever musical skills he possessed. This is the leader-turned-musician.

At the outset, the leader-turned-musician might not possess much musical ability. If he has any musical background, he might further develop those skills and become a more well-rounded worship leader. Or, he might shift from worship ministry to other areas if more musically gifted leaders step up. Regardless, the leader-turned-musician fills a void though he may not possess great musical abilities.

In some cases, the leader-turned-musician may lead for many years in spite of limited musical ability. This happens frequently in smaller churches with fewer resources. If the community has a need for a leader-turned-musician, there's usually a lack of musicians in the congregation. Thus, such a leader could continue to serve without growing musically.

Musical limitations pose some of the biggest challenges for the leader-turned-musician. He may be less musical than other congregation members. His singing or playing may distract people during worship. People may even consider him a poor musician. Nevertheless, this leader continues humbly and faithfully since he knows the importance of worship and there is no one else available to fill that role.

What can we do in such cases? The leader-turned-musician should either invest time and resources to develop musically, and/or pray for God to raise up another leader more suited for worship ministry. Sometimes the biggest contribution of leader-turned-musician is to fill a gap until God provides other workers. This is true for any ministry: There will always be those who have a genuine heart of service and a willingness to fill a need until someone better suited comes along. At that time, the humble servant should gladly pass on the music ministry to those better suited. (That's why I'm not leading worship anymore!)

But if the less-musical leader continues to lead worship in spite of the availability of more musical leaders, then problems can begin to occur. When people's gifts don't match up with the right ministries, those gifts are not fully utilized. This can result in people feeling like they aren't serving as God intended because they are unable to step into the role they have been gifted in. After a prolonged period, such musicians may leave a church because they want to be in a church where they can more fully exercise their gifts.

This is true for all gifts and talents. For example, gifted evangelists become restless or frustrated if they feel they are not maximizing their God-given talents. In order to use their gifts, they will gravitate toward a church that values evangelism more, even if it means leaving one church for another. This also happens with those gifted with administration, teaching, or any other ministry. (I am not condoning or condemning this. I am just pointing out that it happens. Ideally, spiritual gifts match the ministry one serves in.) In those situations, the leader-turned-musician should discern this happening and graciously step aside to allow those more gifted to take up this ministry. This usually redirects the leader-turned-musician to where he can make a greater impact as well.

Barnabas provides an example of this when he called Saul of Tarsus to join their preaching team (Acts 9:26:30). Initially their team was known as "Barnabas and Saul." Barnabas was a very good preacher. But Barnabas gladly raised up Saul who was a great preacher. As Saul's preaching gifts developed—and as he changed his name to Paul—their team became "Paul and Barnabas" (Acts 13).

The Musician-Turned-Leader

The musician-turned-leader sees himself as a musician who leads worship. In my experience, a musician-turned-leader often starts to serve on worship team before he is spiritually ready. In some cases, he may not even be a professing Christian. (For some, this is not an issue. For others, being a Christian is a requirement for worship leading. See Chapter Four on "Talent or Maturity?") In many cases, these people started leading worship because of their musical abilities. These folks enjoyed playing music and were open to using their gifts for the worship ministry. They might have been just as happy to use their musical gifts in other areas, such as accompanying the choir or making musical offertories.

It might have started in a conversation after church when someone said, "Our worship team needs a new piano player since Christine is moving away."

"How about Fred? I think he plays the piano."

"Does he play the drums? We sure could use a drummer."

"He doesn't. But I heard Bill and Sue's son, Jeremy,

plays the drums."

"Great! You ask Fred to play piano and I'll ask Jeremy if he'd be willing to play drums for worship team."

"But I'm not sure if Jeremy is even a Christian..."

There's nothing wrong with this type of conversation when looking for potential worship team members. But this thinking shows how people first look for musical ability, and second for spiritual maturity. It's important to recognize that an accomplished musician might not be a spiritually mature leader.

Just like the leader-turned-musician may have limited musical abilities, the musician-turned-leader may have limited leadership abilities. With training and encouragement, he might become a mature Christian leader over time. If so, then he will become a more well-rounded worship leader. But often, this volunteer who excels in music lacks sufficient spiritual maturity. In fact, his spiritual life may be poor or nonexistent.

Some might object, saying, "No one's perfect. And it's not like he's preaching. He's just leading worship." But that line of reasoning misses the point.

Worship leaders exercise spiritual leadership. They choose the songs we sing every week. They model lives of worship. They are often the first people on the platform during the service that newcomers see. They serve the role of directing our hearts and minds upon the living God. How can we say "It's not like he's preaching. He's just leading worship,"? Rather, we should say, "While no one is perfect, God does have a higher standard for those in spiritual leadership or influence (James 3:1). If Levites and priests are the Old Testament versions of worship leaders, then we should never think "He's *just* leading worship."

A musician-turned-leader must understand the demands of spiritual leadership. A musician-turned-leader influences the spiritual life and direction of the congregation just as surely as a teaching pastor does. The congregation will look to the worship leader as a model of worship. A musician-turned-leader must appreciate how he serves in a visible, public role. People in the community will recognize this musician as the worship leader at the local church. A musician-turned-leader must live with integrity. If a musician-turned-leader excels musically but does not grow spiritually, then his leadership falters. People will not follow his lead in song if they feel they cannot follow his lead in life. We must understand that musical abilities alone do not make a great worship leader. Instead, a great musician must grow in spiritual leadership and Christian maturity.

Teach Artists To Lead, Teach Art To Leaders

All worship leaders must grow in both art and leadership. We must provide training appropriate to our worship leaders so they can develop both their art and their leadership skills. We must teach spiritual leadership to the musician-turned-leader and train musical artistry to the leader-turned-musician.

For leaders who want to develop their art, I offer these suggestions:

- Hone your musical craft. You are a musician, not just a leader.

- Master the musical basics of tempo, pitch, and the fundamental skills for your instrument (including your singing voice).

- Ask the more musical team members to suggest ways to improve the music or song arrangements.

- When not leading, be a good "off-stage leader." You may not be on the platform, but the congregation is watching you. Be on time and participate in worship, especially when you are not leading worship. Do not be a hypocritical worship leader who appears fully engaged when leading, but then arrives late when not leading.
- Support the team, model engagement in worship, and look out for ways to grow.

For artists who want to develop their leadership, I offer these suggestions:

- Hone your spiritual leadership, for you are a leader, not just a musician. Ask your pastor or some other appropriate leader to offer your mentoring or resources. Seek out someone who can disciple you in the areas of leadership. Humbly acknowledge that musical ability is not enough for effective worship leading.
- Master the leadership essentials of organizing your team, public prayer, and submitting to your congregation and pastor.
- When not leading, engage musically even if the music sounds substandard to you. Do not be a hypocritical worship leader who tells people to be expressive when he leads yet is not expressive when he follows others.
- Invite your spiritually mature team members to suggest ways you can improve your character and leadership.

- Support the team, model engagement in worship, and look out for ways to grow.

How About You?

If you're reading this book, you probably lead worship (or work with those who do). You would do well to understand your own path. Did your journey in worship ministry begin as a leader-turned-musician or as a musician-turned-leader? The more you see what you are, the better you can develop yourself and others around you.

WORKBOOK

Chapter Three Questions

Your Heart: Are you naturally an artist or a leader? How did you get started in leading worship, and is this a role that you see as a full-time profession, a temporary voluntary service, or something in-between? In what ways can you grow in either your musical abilities (if you are naturally a leader), or in your spiritual leadership (if you are naturally an artist)?

_____

_____

_____

_____

_____

_____

_____

_____

_____

Your Church: Does your church value leadership or artistry more? How can the church support its leaders in becoming better artists, and its artists in becoming better leaders? (e.g., paying for training or conferences; initiating mentoring and discipleship, etc.)

_____
_____
_____
_____
_____
_____
_____
_____
_____
_____

Your Commitment: Do a study on verses in Scripture that speak to the importance of spiritual leadership (see, as a starting point, the descriptions of a disciple in the Sermon on the Mount, the fruit of the Spirit in Galatians 5, and the qualifications for church leaders in 1 Timothy 3:1–7). Then look at verses that speak to the importance of skill, artistry, and doing one's best (see 1 Corinthians 10:31; Colossians 3:23 and Psalm 33:3 as a starting point, as well as the descriptions of the tabernacle and temple). What steps will you take to develop in the areas where you are lacking and to reinforce those where you are naturally gifted?

_____
_____
_____
_____
_____
_____
_____
_____
_____
_____

Chapter Three Notes

PART ONE: TEAM

Chapter Four:
Competency or Character?

The tension between musical competency and spiritual character is real. As discussed in Chapter Three, we should not spiritualize resolving the tension with clichés like "It's all about the heart."

Would you want an untrained preacher, bus driver, or surgeon? Most likely, no. In the same manner, we should look for worship leaders with talent and abilities as well as spiritual character.

But if a choice must be made between the two, which one is more important? Spiritual character or musical competency?

I've heard many Christians say that character trumps competency. I agree that in much of life, your character (maturity) matters more than your competency (musical ability). I'd rather a spouse be faithful than have a successful career. I'd rather my children have integrity than excel in school.

But I think such a question oversimplifies the solution. Don't we hope to have both? And in ministry, I think it's a mistake to say that all a leader needs is character. A leader really needs both character and competency.

In other words, worship leaders must meet musical qualifications *as well as* spiritual qualifications.

But isn't it easier to build competency than character? After all, it's easier to teach someone how to sing than to make a selfish person generous, right? Again, I think this oversimplifies the issue.

The Bible teaches that those who serve God should possess both spiritual and technical qualifications. The apostle James writes that preachers should possess the maturity required of their stricter standard (James 3:1), and the apostle Paul taught that teachers should also possess the gifts and skills of teaching (Romans 12:6–7).

Healthy churches must not fall prey to choosing character at the expense of competency and vice versa. We must strive for both competency and character.

Here's how I've observed this work out. Let's imagine a small church with a middle-aged pastor. He values commitment and maturity. His people appreciate quality preaching and music, of course. But they've come to appreciate the heart of the leaders. They might prioritize character over competency. So, in looking for a new worship leader, the pastor might make a list of people who are spiritually mature. He asks, "Who is spiritually mature enough for this job?" Then he'll look over that list and identify the people with the most gifts. That's the person he'll aim to recruit.

Take another common occurrence. Let's imagine a leader of a campus ministry at a local college. He's young and passionate. He also knows that to reach the campus, he needs to have quality music that connects with college-aged students. He's looking for a worship leader. So, he lists all the people in his ministry who are gifted musicians and charismatic leaders. He asks, "Who can do a great job?" He looks over his list and tries to pick the person who is also the most mature in his faith.

I realize these are stereotypes. But I often find that there is a bit of truth in some (not all) stereotypes. I did not make any of these examples up. I've seen each of these play out numerous times.

These leaders logically identify leaders. They want leaders who have maturity and ability, so they screen for their most important qualification first. For example, they set character as the higher quality. Then they filter that list through the second qualification, in this example, ability.

This is logical, but I think it falls prey to the false dichotomy that leaders in smaller ministries have to choose either spiritual character or musical competency. I think you can get both. This takes time and potentially years of investment. But I believe God wants you to have both and will bring the correct leader to your ministry in His perfect timing.

When seeking out potential leaders, I don't screen first for maturity or ability. Instead, I ask this question: Which potential leaders do I see God at work in?

Sometimes it's a leader with great competency but immature character. Such a person may be young, brash, or impulsive. But with a caring, godly mentor, they can grow.

Sometimes I see a leader with great heart and low ability. It may seem unlikely to hope this person becomes skilled at music. But with opportunity, encouragement, and time, they can excel. As an equipper you are called to equip people in whatever they lack.

I have not found a simple rule to always choose correctly between spiritual character or musical competency. But I have found it worthwhile to invest in both kinds of people: those with skill who need to grow spiritually, and those with maturity who need to grow musically.

Whoever you identify to invest in, give them what you can to develop both them both as leaders and musicians.

The choice to develop the spiritually mature individual

or the musically talented individual may depend on the strengths of you or your church. If you do a great job teaching music, then perhaps you should take mature leaders and help them develop musically. If you have a great track record with discipling or mentoring, perhaps you should take musicians who are humble and teachable to help them develop maturity.

No matter who you develop, you should balance the depth of both character and competency. But as you develop people, you will find that the pool of people to choose from in your church may change over time.

What if a church tries and just cannot seem to find people with both the character and the competency for certain roles, such as worship leaders? My response is "it depends." At the time I am writing this, we have access to musical tools that we could not have imagined a generation ago. We can acquire sound tracks or videos designed to help us sing along in corporate worship. Some churches may find this "worship by karaoke" awkward or distasteful. Those churches may feel demoralized that they cannot field a suitably qualified worship team. Yet using technology to aid us may be a good option for some situations.

Another way to address a shortage of suitable leaders inside a church is to explore finding a quality candidate outside the church. This may mean recruiting Christian worship leaders from local colleges or asking larger churches in the area for help with training. In some cases, a church may consider creating a paid position. Larger churches may be more able to sustain hiring worship leaders. Churches who may have fewer financial resources may consider investing those resources in bringing in outside help to train up those in their church.

If a church chooses to bring in someone from the outside, it's preferable that such a person can not only perform the tasks, but ideally would be capable of training up and equipping others in those tasks as well.

Balance and Lift

We really have two goals in raising up worship teams. First, we want to balance out requirements, such as spiritual character and technical competency. But that's not our only goal. As our second goal, we also want to raise the levels of both character and competency in our teams. I describe this process as "balance and lift." We balance the needs of spiritual character and musical competency *while* we lift levels of character and competency.

In other words, look for people who are the most spiritually qualified and the most musically capable. And then do everything you can to grow them in character and in competency.

Why do we need both goals of balancing character and competency, while also lifting the bar of leadership? Because in smaller churches, you may not find individuals with both character and skill. And even if you do, it's less likely to find a deeply mature and highly skilled leader in smaller churches. If you have those, feel grateful. You are the exception. Most smaller churches, especially ones with an ethnic heritage such as Asian American, have a lack of qualified leaders within them.

This is not a criticism of smaller churches or ministries. It's just a statistical reality. In most cases, the more people you have in a church, the more people you have to draw from for various ministry roles. This increases the chances you have of people who have both competency and character.

If looking strictly within your church, I suggest you identify those who are most qualified to be leaders and who have the best balance of character and competency that fits your needs. But don't just deploy them. Develop them. They may be your best leaders, but they can still benefit from further development and coaching.

For parachurch groups such as ministries on college

campuses, worship teams are at the mercy of the student population for that year. Some years you've got spiritually mature musicians aplenty. Other years, you can't even find someone who can keep a beat, let alone sing in tune. Such ministries tend to take and deploy workers who come with prior experience. You can and should work at developing leaders, but a school year goes by fast. While students may have more flexible time to develop, you have less time in the course of the year to develop them. But in churches and other year-round ministries, we may have people who have full-time jobs and less availability to develop, but they have more time overall to develop into leaders over multiple years.

If you want to develop your worship ministry—either the musical aspect or the leadership aspect—you will need to break through to greater levels of both technical and spiritual leadership. I find that if you do a good job balancing musical competence with spiritual character, you're most of the way toward lifting the ministry to new heights. That's because people thrive when they are well matched to ministry roles by spiritual character and competency.

Lifting the Bar: The Problem with Progress

Let's say God blesses the ministry and the church grows. That brings in not only more worshipers, but also more potential worship leaders. This is good, but it presents new challenges.

Here's a typical scenario: a faithful worship team has been leading during a season of numeric growth. With growth comes more people and potential workers. And with more potential workers, the greater the chance that there are more gifted people in that mix. You may find that your congregation has attracted musicians with more skill than what you've had before.

Now let's say some of those higher caliber musicians are also mature and experienced worship leaders. Not only that, they express interest in serving in worship ministry. You now face a challenging but predictable situation. If you take in the newer leaders who have more talent and ability, they may "squeeze" out your faithful servants who can no longer keep up musically. But if you don't take in those newer, more talented leaders, your ministry might not develop as God wants you to develop it.

You want to honor and appreciate those faithful servants who have served in the worship ministry so far. But you also want to take the ministry to new levels. What do you do? Do you let current leaders continue even though God has brought in more gifted individuals? Do you remove current leaders to make room for more gifted ones?

Most people dislike the idea of removing current leaders just because there are new people with greater character or competency. But this is a crucial leadership test for the ministry and the church. Is there biblical precedent on this? Well, I think we can see a biblical precedent when a talented leader voluntarily moves aside to make way for an even more talented leader in the case of Barnabas and Saul.

Barnabas Makes Way for Saul

The Bible contains a scenario with this very issue with Barnabas and Saul in Acts 11:22–26. Barnabas was a respected leader in the early church. Eventually, Barnabas came to Antioch where the ministry flourished under his leadership and preaching. But when he saw the hunger of the Antioch church for God's Word, he went to get a man named Saul to come and preach.

While Barnabas was a very good preacher, Paul apparently was a great preacher. The time came when God said he wanted to send out missionaries from this church. So, they set aside Barnabas and Saul. When they left on their mission trip in Acts 13, the team was known as "Barnabas and Saul." But soon after they left, the team was no longer "Barnabas and Saul." Saul would change his name to Paul, and they were known as "Paul and Barnabas." (Acts 13–15).

What had happened? Paul's gifts and leadership had surpassed Barnabas's. So, what did Barnabas do? He voluntarily stepped aside and let Paul continue to exercise his gifts.

I believe Barnabas did this intentionally. It happens best when the current leader seeks to replace himself with someone more gifted than himself. And it also works best when the newer, more gifted leader is gracious, humble, and patient.

Leaders Who Surpass Us

I would love it if the leaders who follow me surpass me in every way. I would love it if my children surpassed me in wisdom, love, and godliness. I pray God will give me the grace to pass the mantle of leadership to the next generation when the time comes. And I pray God will not let me overstay my time in leadership positions!

I have gotten in trouble when I have shared this concept with people. As the worship ministry developed in my church, we had to become more selective with those whom we chose. People who would have been selected in years past might not have the gifting needed to join the ministry today. I know this sounds snobby, ungrateful, and elitist to some, and I have learned to better articulate my view on this. But after much thought and prayer and Bible study, I still believe this to be the Bible's teaching. We should ask God for wisdom in the timing and application of being more selective as our ministries grow. And we should be seeking His will in each stage of the worship team and leadership's development and growth.

So, as you identify leaders for your worship ministry, or any ministry for that matter, remember the Bible teaches that leaders should possess both character and competency, as I have explained in my discussion on James 3:1 and Romans 12:6-7 above. You may not find leaders with both qualifications initially, so you must prepare to invest the time, energy, and resources to develop them. And may the leaders you invest in eventually surpass you in every way for the glory of God.

WORKBOOK

Chapter Four Questions

Your Heart: Are you stagnant or growing in your spiritual character and your musical competency? Do you crave the attention and honor of your ministry, or do you see yourself as a servant to develop new worship leaders who will surpass you?

_____
_____
_____
_____
_____
_____
_____
_____

Your Church: List some ways can you help each member of your team to grow in both character and competency. (Some things may be ideas that will help the entire team to grow, while others may be for a certain individual.) How can you help foster an attitude among the team that encourages each to do their best and grow, but also an attitude that welcomes new talent and is even willing to "step aside" when the time is right?

_____
_____
_____
_____
_____
_____
_____
_____
_____
_____

Your Commitment: Write out or journal your vision for the worship leaders currently on your team. How would you like to see each individual grow (both in character and competency)? Be specific. Ask "Who is God working in?" and pray for wisdom to identify new leaders. Next, describe your vision for the leader(s) who will eventually surpass and replace you. How can your ministry today be a stepping stone for those who will follow after you?

Chapter Four Notes

PART ONE: TEAM

Chapter Five:
Best Practices for Better Songs

In addition to spiritual character and musical competency, it is also imperative that a worship leader be organized and structured. This largely comes into play when setting up team practices.

Why should we consider best practices for team practices? Because if we don't, we may hold team practices that frustrate team members, use up people's precious time, and miss opportunities to develop our worship leaders.

Frankly, I have seen many worship team members in smaller churches step down from the worship teams out of frustration about poorly run rehearsals. These are some of the problems with poorly run rehearsals people have shared with me over the years:

- Team members arrive late or leave early, which means other team members may end up feeling like they are wasting their time waiting.
- Instrumentalists spend time working out a complicated musical phrase while the vocalists just

sit there looking at their phones.
- The team leader does not come prepared with music, or the music is not in the right key.

If you are the worship team leader, one of the most important responsibilities you have is to bring your best effort in making worship practice productive, efficient, and enjoyable. That begins by considering basic matters about your worship team rehearsals.

When Is the Best Date and Time to Rehearse?

When is the best time for your worship team to practice? Most people don't ask this basic question when planning out their worship schedule. Often, that's because they inherited a rehearsal schedule or culture from a previous leader. "Our worship practices are on Tuesday evenings because... well, they've been on Tuesday evenings for as long as anyone can remember!"

I suggest that your practice times should meet two requirements. First, pick a time that works best for your team. Don't set rehearsal time when your team members are too tired or stressed. You cannot get the perfect time for everybody, but if people are continually late or distracted or irritable, then step back and check for a better rehearsal time.

Second, pick a time close to the actual worship event. A shorter time between rehearsal and the worship service helps your team remember what you've practiced. If your team is up to play on Sunday morning, then practices on Friday or Saturday work best. They end the practice knowing that in a day (or two), they'll probably still remember what they just practiced. But if your team practices on Monday night for an upcoming Sunday, they have to remember the arrangements for an entire week.

Another option is to schedule the rehearsal on the day

of the worship service, but early enough to run through everything and also have time for a brief break. This works well if the musicians are skillful enough and confident enough to pull this off. However, in my experience, in smaller churches where we may find a shortage of capable musicians, rehearsing on the day of service may be too stressful for some people. In that case, practicing a day or two before the worship service provides the team a bit more time to polish up the songs on their own.

Consider each worship team individually. I have led worship teams where we rehearsed earlier in the week *and* ran through the full set before the service, and they *still* felt anxious about playing the songs. I have also led worship teams where different people did not know the songs or who else would be playing that day until they arrived. This was a team of professionally trained musicians who were very comfortable with coming in an hour before the service and could be ready within that time.

Both of these teams were in the same church, on alternating Sundays!

Someone might say, "My team practices many days ahead because they need more practice to be ready." If that's your situation, I suggest you pick easier songs. If your team can't play a song well by the end of rehearsal, you'll need another rehearsal for when the entire team can play the song properly. Worship service is too important to lead songs your team can't yet play well. Save such songs for after your team can play them confidently and skillfully. I will discuss this matter further in Chapter Ten.

Budget Time to Set Up and Clean Up

When you ask your worship team to practice, clarify if you expect them to be ready to play music at that time. If you expect them to be ready to play music at the appointed time, you're really asking that they show up earlier to set up their respective instruments. You also need to ensure that any sound equipment needed is ready.

I prefer to plan rehearsal time to include both setup and cleanup. For example, if rehearsal starts at 7 p.m., I don't plan to start music until 7:30 p.m. And if we are scheduled to end rehearsal at 9:30 p.m., then I plan to end music playing by 9 p.m. so we have 30 minutes to clean up.

If you rehearse in the venue of your service and can leave your gear set up, it will save you much time and energy. But many of us do not have that luxury. Many churches and campus groups must transport, set up, and break down all their gear each rehearsal.

If a rehearsal looks like it will run long, offer to stay late so you can release team members at the appointed ending time. If people consistently arrive late or you still don't have enough practice time, then evaluate the root cause. You may want to consider a new practice time or location. Or you may have a deeper issue about team morale, team commitment, or time management.

A Typical Rehearsal in My Church

For my teams, a typical rehearsal might go something like this:

- *Set Up*: Set up system, instruments (20 minutes)
- *Prayer*: Gather in a circle (away from the instruments) for prayer and any prayer items that people are preoccupied with (10 minutes)
- *Talk Through*: Talk through song set (still away from the instruments), noting dynamics, number of times through verses, choruses, etc. (10 minutes)

- *Rehearse Songs*: Practice songs (approx. 60 minutes for 6–7 songs)
- *Rehearse Transitions*: Practice transitions between songs (approx. 30 minutes for 6–7 songs)
- *Break Down*: Break-down gear and clean up (20 minutes)
- *Total Time*: 150 minutes

Our practice takes longer because in my church, we have to set up and clean up the sound system and drum kit each time.

The worship team, and especially the team leader, should plan rehearsal times so as to make the most of people's time and honor their schedules. When planning your worship practice, here are a few things to keep in mind.

1. Leaders should have music planned in advance. As a leader, you should always have the songs you plan to use for the service picked out in advance of practice. Few things frustrate a worship team more than showing up to find the leader has not yet selected all the songs. Such procrastination smacks of disorganized and inconsiderate leadership. When rehearsal begins, leaders should have sufficient copies of song sheets for the team and the song sheets should have the correct lyrics and music.

2. Leaders should be ready to sing, play, and lead songs. It's not enough to come to rehearsal having picked your songs, however. You should practice the songs in advance. Rehearsal is time for the team—not the leader—to learn the songs. The leader should be ready to teach any new songs to the team.

3. Leaders should order and arrange the songs ahead of time. The leader should come with a plan for the arrangement of each song and all the songs in the set. (More on this in Chapter Thirteen on "Set Flow.") Of course, leaders should be flexible and adapt based on team input. But that's no excuse for the leader not to plan song arrangements beforehand.

A leader should have practiced enough to select dynamics, tempo, and key for each song. Remember to arrange songs according to your team and congregational situation. (We'll get to this in Parts 2 and 3 of this book.) Do all this before rehearsal.

4. Leaders should prep the team before playing music. A few minutes of preparation before actually playing music can save many minutes during the rehearsal. Prepare the team by sending songs out before practice. Send them the music sheets, notes on your proposed arrangements, and if legal, the actual song in video or audio format, such as via a link to an arrangement you saw on YouTube or another website.

I like to buy the song and make or purchase enough legal copies to give to my team in a suitable audio format, like MP3s. This small gift shows my appreciation to the team, and it ensures they'll have plenty of opportunity to familiarize themselves with the song if it's loaded on their music players.

Some alternatives may be creating a playlist using Spotify, which may be more accessible to a wider range of people. There is also a tool called Planning Center, which enables you to create schedules, attach sheet music documents, and link websites for audio or video of the songs, etc. Different tools, apps, and services are constantly changing, so do some research and ask other worship leaders in other churches.

Of course, teams with skilled musicians might not need

as much preparation. They might be able to play a song after hearing it a time or two. However, the general principle is this: The less experienced the team, the more preparation they need before rehearsal. During one season of my ministry, my team consisted mostly of professional musicians or music majors. All the preparation they needed would be to listen to the songs on the way to rehearsal. When I worked with less musical folks, they appreciated getting songs many days in advance to practice. Do what best serves your team and situation.

5. Leaders should invite team feedback. A good worship team leader invites feedback. He invites feedback on the song selection, the musical arrangement, and the actual leading.

Explain your song arrangement to your team. Then play it and see how it goes. Adjust based on team feedback. In my experience, suggestions from my teams usually resulted in better arrangements.

6. Leaders don't force a song to work. If your team isn't confident about playing a song, don't force it. Even if it's the "perfect song" to go with a sermon—even if a world-famous preacher requested the song—if your team isn't ready, don't do it. Why lead a song that your team can't play well? Why risk distracting worshipers with shaky music? If you can't play the "perfect song" properly, it's not the perfect song.

If you're coming close to the end of a practice and still haven't rehearsed that new song, beware of thinking, "We'll practice that song on Sunday morning before service." Worship teams should be able to confidently play their songs. Just go with a song your team can already play and do the new song another time.

Start and End Practice with Prayer

We don't have to over-spiritualize rehearsal. If you want to budget into your rehearsal an extended time of prayer, sharing prayer requests, or Bible study, go right ahead. But if all you have time to do each rehearsal is to practice, that's fine. I find that the smaller the church and/or team, the more the team tends to focus on relationships. But the larger the ministry and/or team, the more a team focuses on the job of preparing to lead worship. That's because in smaller churches, people know most people better than in larger churches. In a large church with many musicians, a team may practice together and not even know each other's names!

That being said, you are preparing not just your voices and instruments, but also your minds and hearts. Start and end rehearsals with prayer as appropriate.

Everyone's a "Roadie"

I co-led the worship team for our church's high school group years ago. During those practices we instilled the importance of proper care and storage of all the gear. On one occasion, we were teaching how to properly wrap and store audio cables. One of the senior-year team members protested, saying, "I didn't join worship team to wrap up cables!"

My co-leader smiled and replied, "Oh yes, you did," and handed the teenager a cable to wrap.

In the music industry, a "roadie" is someone who takes care of the sound gear. It's hard work that involves moving heavy equipment, arriving early to set up the sound system, and staying late to put gear away. But people like the opportunity to travel with their band on tour.

Most of our churches will not have professional or hired roadies. So, we train everybody on our worship teams to help out. That is, we train them with the skills to properly situate and lay out gear. We also instill the work ethic to help the sound people when we can.

We also have some rules for worship team practice. Everybody helps set up. The drum kit takes more time and work to set up, so our vocalists learned how to set up the drums and cymbals. The piano was usually already in the room, so pianists helped set up microphones and music stands. We emphasized that worship team members should all pitch in to set up and break down. At the very least, they should offer to help. It's not their fault if the drummer doesn't want anyone to touch his gear!

Special Circumstances: Retreats and the Pre-Set Rehearsal

If you're practicing before a worship set at a retreat, time is scarce. In many smaller churches, worship teams give up their precious retreat time to rehearse for worship. As a pastor in smaller churches, I appreciate their dedication. But I prefer they spend time at retreats in fellowship, prayer, or rest rather than worship practice.

Here are my suggestions for these situations. First, don't practice worship sets. Instead, practice a repertoire of songs. Retreats call for flexibility. Instead of practicing three sets of four songs each, I will prepare a repertoire of ten songs. Then before the worship session, I will determine my order of songs. This gives me freedom to make changes because I know my team can play any of the songs I may choose from our repertoire.

Second, do not practice the songs. Instead, practice the transitions between songs. Just as the most crucial part of flying a plane is during takeoff and landing, so the times when worship teams trip up is at the start or the end of a song.

Practice the intro so that you're clean and tight. Then

practice the outro. Get that ending clean and clear. Practice any transitions within the songs, such as to a tricky bridge or repeat. But avoid playing the entire song. Your team should be fine, assuming you've practiced enough before the retreat. Save the team time and save the vocalists their voices to enjoy the rest of the retreat.

In conclusion, healthy worship teams usually have great rehearsals. What a blessing to the team if they look forward to rehearsals in which they can prepare, play music, and enjoy worshiping God together. When the worship team members enjoy worshiping God together, then they will likely better guide the congregation in worship. So, better worship team rehearsals directly impact the quality of worship in our services.

WORKBOOK

Chapter Five Questions

Your Heart: Evaluate your personal commitment to your rehearsals. Are you investing adequate time and energy into praying, planning, and preparing for each rehearsal?

_____
_____
_____
_____
_____
_____
_____
_____
_____
_____
_____

Your Church: Does your team value and honor their rehearsal time? Are there team members who are consistently late or unprepared, and if so, are there logistical changes that could help them to be more faithful? If your team seems to be ambivalent about rehearsals, consider a group conversation or even an anonymous survey to hear their thoughts about what is going well and what needs improvement for your rehearsals. Evaluate if any confrontation or corrective action needs to be made.

_____

_____

_____

_____

_____

_____

_____

_____

_____

_____

Your Commitment: Using the evaluations above as well as the guidelines in this chapter, write out a detailed schedule for your next rehearsal. Make copies available to each team member well in advance of the rehearsal. If you have not already, choose a consistent time each week that you will pray, plan, and prepare for that week's rehearsal.

In Reverence and Awe

_____
_____
_____
_____
_____
_____
_____
_____
_____
_____

Chapter Five Notes

PART ONE: TEAM

Chapter Six:
Raising Teams

Supposedly over half of the Protestant churches in the US have less than 100 people.[1] In my experience, churches of that size are called "smaller" churches, but that label seems to be unhelpful. If this range is the most common size, maybe they should be called "normal" churches.

And yet many of the people who write helpful books on leading worship come from larger ministries. I've benefited from many of those books, but I also have a burden to encourage worship leaders in a smaller church setting. In the following paragraphs, I share thoughts about raising worship teams in both a smaller congregation and a larger congregation.

Smaller Churches with Bigger Challenges

Have you found it challenging to raise up a worship team in a smaller church with few or no musicians? Consider the constraints the worship leader has in a small church or ministry:

- There are few or no obvious musicians.
- You have little or no budget for instruments.
- There's little interest or expertise to maintain or upgrade the sound system.
- Volunteers already are involved in too many other ministries.
- People compare your ministry to that of the regional megachurch.

The smaller the congregation, generally the fewer available musicians there are to choose from. With fewer musicians to choose from, the congregation's expectations might not be as high as attendees of a larger church. This is both a help and a hindrance.

It's a help because people may be content with whatever limited musical abilities are present in the congregation. But this can also hinder because people are less likely to try to break through to higher levels of musical excellence.

This happens for two reasons. First, people may be satisfied with the music and don't see a need to improve it. After all, people usually come to small churches for the tight-knit community, not the music.

Second, people who are more musical than the current level of worship music will probably seek churches where musical excellence is more valued. So, while lower standards mean people are more easily satisfied by the music, lower standards also mean it's harder to take the worship ministry to higher levels.

Invest in Who You Have

My advice is do the best with what you have. If all you

have is one pianist who plays a shaky accompaniment, then glorify God in that. Balance the current musical resources with the spiritual leadership resources. (See the section "Balance Then Lift" in Chapter Four, entitled "Character or Competency.")

But by all means, lift that balance up as much as you can. Invest in musicians, especially the younger ones. Musicians who are children or youth often have more time to practice their instruments. (They also learn faster.) You may find younger people are more receptive and more teachable than adults. The insecure middle school student strumming shaky guitar chords today may be a competent musician and maturing worship leader in a few years.

Invest in them even if it means letting them play on the team for some time though they aren't quite up to the level of others.

In smaller ministries, that may be the best way to learn. Take them on. Invite them to your band practices. If they're not ready to lead with the worship team on stage, they can still participate in rehearsals. Give them music recordings (purchased legally) to inspire them to improve musically. Give them sermon recordings to challenge them spiritually. Consider using church funds (or your own) to buy a starter guitar or a drum set or electric piano/organ. And then pray for them.

It's a matter of numbers. The larger the church, the more potential worship leaders. The larger the number of potential worship leaders, the greater chances that there are more skillful musicians among them. The more skillful musicians, the sooner you can build up a ministry. For example, a church with a large college ministry will more likely find spiritually qualified and musically capable volunteers than a church with virtually no students.

So, if you're in a smaller church and want to develop the future worship ministry (or any ministry for that matter), invest heavily in the future. Lather encouragement on the younger generation. Paint a picture that your current students might serve and grow in this church for many years to come. If students go away for college, plant the idea of them coming back on breaks and after graduation. Just be careful to do so without laying inappropriate guilt on them, especially in Asian American contexts.

Pray to the Lord that young people find local jobs so that they can stay in the church family. A strength of the smaller congregation is the close-knit relationships among the members. Use that close-knit dynamic to invest in future worship leaders, as well as future Sunday school teachers, deacons, elders, and pastors.

What About the Adults?

You may have noticed I haven't mentioned teaching the adults in your church to learn to play musical instruments. If they can do that, by all means, support that. But I have rarely seen an adult with little or no musical training have enough time to invest to become competent to play today's worship songs.

Today's worship songs are musically more complex than a few decades ago. Instead of adults learning instruments (and new musical genres and styles), I suggest adults encourage and invest in younger people to lead worship.

Compared to the Megachurch in Town?

Finally, let me address the issue of comparing your worship ministry with that of the bigger church across town. I usually hear people say things like this, "Don't compare yourself with others. They have more resources so it's not fair to compare."

I appreciate the sentiment. But it's more helpful to think a different way.

Go ahead and compare your worship ministry (or any ministry for that matter) with other churches. But compare not to loathe and groan, but to learn and grow. How can we improve if we do not benefit by the positive example of others? Even the Apostle Paul compared different churches and ministry leaders to highlight a positive example to follow. (See 2 Cor 9:1-5; 11:7-10.) A godly spirit of comparison instructs and benefits us, but worldly comparison belittles and discourages us.

So, compare, but compare with a healthy perspective. Compare not with writhing and humiliation, but with wisdom and humility. Compare with a teachable spirit that is willing to do the hard work to develop.

Larger Churches with Larger Problems

It may surprise you that larger churches also struggle with raising teams. Some challenges they face are similar to those of smaller congregations. But larger ministries face their own set of problems, with increasing complexity.

One problem may surprise you: Sometimes there are just too many musicians. I can guess what you are thinking: "What kind of problem is that? I'd love to have the 'problem' of too many musicians!"

It may be hard to imagine, but having more volunteers than ministry opportunities is a problem. There may not be enough service opportunities for all those musicians. Consequently, those people are not fully utilizing their gifts and not leveraging their resources for the Kingdom. If that's not a problem, I don't know what is.

If you have too many volunteers, not only do people not utilize their gifts, but this often leads to people thinking, "I don't need to serve because there are so many people here."

If you've ever served in leadership for a larger church,

you may be nodding your head. This is a big problem. And often, the bigger the church, the bigger this problem.

Larger churches may have plenty of musicians in the congregation, but proportionally few of them are serving in worship ministry. This happens not just because there are proportionally fewer opportunities. It happens because they look around and see what appears to be an unlimited army of volunteers. The result is they decide this church doesn't need them.

This idea that "the church doesn't need me to serve" tends to undervalue the individual Christian's ministry in the local church. That itself is unacceptable. But it gets worse if no one addresses this problem. A larger ministry that does not address this issue will soon find itself feeling crushed by the weight of all the high expectations with fewer workers.

It's a commonly held view—though I've never seen a study on it—that the larger the church, two things will be true. First, the percentage of members actively serving goes down. And second, the level of expectations upon those who serve increases. In other words, the expectations of excellence go up, but the number of willing volunteers goes down. This is a double whammy on larger churches!

Everyone Knows Bill

Consider the small congregation in need of a new worship leader. In a smaller congregation, most people will know about the need. In a small congregation, everyone knows that someone in the group has to fill that need. They will talk among themselves, pray, and consider how to meet the need. When someone does come forward to lead worship (and someone always does, even if they are not musical), everyone else will be grateful. They also know the volunteer personally and appreciate if it's a stretch for the leader.

There's usually more grace in smaller ministries. *"Sure, the vocalist is out of tune, but I know him. That singer is Bill. He teaches my kids in Sunday school. He also sits on the operations team and fixes up the church. Everyone knows Bill. Everyone loves Bill. Everyone knows that Bill hasn't played guitar for over fifteen years since college. And everyone appreciates Bill for volunteering to fill yet another role in the church."*

On the other hand, consider the larger congregation that finds itself with an established worship leader moving away soon. How many people will even know that leader personally? How many people will learn of the need for another leader? How many people will want to take up such a visible role of leading worship for hundreds, maybe thousands of congregants? Perhaps many congregants will expect the next worship leader to be as good, if not better, at worship leading.

A smaller congregation that does not raise up a qualified worship leader will, in most cases, get by. People probably won't leave the church if the musical quality dips. Indeed, they probably did not join that smaller church because of the music. But a larger congregation may find that the attendees have high expectations. Indeed, in a larger church, when a new music minister joins, some attendees may even consider switching churches because of it.

All this talk about people choosing a church based upon the worship music may sound shallow or unspiritual. Maybe so. But in my experience, pastors appreciate how the quality of the music attracts (or turns away) people. They know people decide upon a church based on the music, just like many decide based upon the preaching. Should it be that way? Probably not. But is that reality? I believe it is. And we should recognize the implications.

Challenges and Opportunities

I could summarize these challenges this way. For the smaller church, beware of thinking, "We'll never find anyone to lead." For the larger church, beware of thinking, "We'll always find someone to lead." Leaders in both smaller and larger churches face challenges raising up worship teams; however, these unique challenges also come with unique opportunities. Smaller churches provide opportunities for many people to serve in ways they may be too intimidated to serve in at a larger church. Larger churches with their larger pool of volunteers provide opportunities for people to pursue higher levels of excellence.

WORKBOOK

Chapter Six Questions

Your Heart: What unique challenges have you faced in worship ministry because of the size and expectations of your church? What are some strengths that you appreciate about the size and attitudes of your church? Thank God for the strengths and ask Him to help you learn and grow in areas of challenge.

_____
_____
_____
_____
_____
_____
_____
_____
_____
_____

Your Church: *Smaller church:* Identify young people in your church who are currently learning an instrument or who show interest and talent in music. How can you invest in them and give them opportunities to grow with your worship team?

Larger church: Do your current worship leaders/worship team feel overwhelmed with high expectations and a proportionate lack of volunteers? How can you effectively bring in new people who may have assumed that they were not needed? How can you prize excellence while keeping a heart focused on worship rather than mere performance?

_____
_____
_____
_____
_____
_____
_____
_____
_____
_____

Your Commitment: If you are in a smaller church, what is a local or semi-local megachurch that you can compare your music to with wisdom and humility? That is, how can you learn from their example and use it as inspiration for your own worship? Consider reaching out to the worship leader at that church to see if he or she can provide any advice or resources to help as you seek to improve the quality of worship at your own church.

If you are in a larger church, consider how you might bless a smaller church in your area by sharing extra resources (music, instruments, decorations) and volunteers. Not that all smaller churches have lower musical quality! But if you're in a larger church, you may have people who feel "unneeded" and may be a blessing to other churches as they share their musical ability to provide occasional support or special music for a congregation without many talented musicians.

Chapter Six Notes

PART ONE: TEAM

Chapter Seven:
My Experience in Building Worship Teams

I grew up in the Asian American Church. Specifically, I grew up in a couple of Chinese-heritage churches—that is, churches that have a Chinese-heritage for the founders and history. In the few Chinese-heritage churches in which I've served, I was in the top echelon of musicians. I used to take sinful pride in this. Now I think this is sad. It's sad not only because pride is wrong, but also because this revealed more about the lack of worship musicians in Chinese-heritage churches than my great musical skill.

Most Asian heritage churches I knew growing up would have been considered small with very few, if any, serviceable musicians for worship. Sure, tons of Chinese Americans took piano and violin lessons over the years, but that was all classical stuff. A small portion might play guitar, and almost no one played drums, unless it was the tympani in honor orchestra. That did not help with the chord-playing, improvisational, contemporary complex music that makes up much of today's worship music.

Most of my experience among east Asian churches is

from Chinese-heritage and Korean-heritage churches. In my experience, there are much fewer evangelical churches of other Asian heritages, such as Vietnamese or Filipino. This probably has to do with the number of people immigrating from those various regions. Moreover, of course, different sections of the US have different concentrations of ethnic groups.

In my experience, Filipinos and Vietnamese groups tend to be more expressive in their worship styles than Chinese or Koreans. This also seems to fit what others have observed.[2]

Worship Music: Past and Present

When I was learning to play guitar for worship, you could play the majority of contemporary worship songs on guitar with just three chords—usually D, A, and G. If you could play a bar chord, you were practically a professional. And if you could play songs in the key of E with chords like B, F#m, and the dreaded C#m without a guitar capo, people considered you a virtuoso.

Today, the typical worship song has four to seven chords, and that's if you don't do a key change.

When I was younger, it was possible to play all the worship songs with a single guitar strum. That's the strum known affectionately as *down-down-up—up-down-up*. At least that's what we call it today. Back then, since it was the only strum we knew, it was called "the strum." But I can't think of a well-known worship song written in the past ten years that uses that strum. And the strums we use today are more complicated and syncopated.

It used to be only megachurches that had the artists and bands to compose worship songs. Today, every church plant seems to feel the pressure to launch worship services with a full band. And the bands are expected to play as well as those performing in the professional recordings we can listen to or watch online. This is hard enough, especially in Asian American contexts where most people played instruments for an orchestra instead of a garage band.

Chinese Americans and Singing

Cultural background can have a significant impact on worship in a church. In southern California, where I grew up, there *were* Asian American churches with musicians. In these churches, it seemed to me that every guy could play guitar, and every girl could sing. I learned a word to describe these churches: Korean.

Besides the scarcity of instrumentalists, Chinese American ministries also faced another challenge: many Chinese Americans don't sing.

As a Chinese American, I grew up learning piano and violin. My parents forced me to learn these instruments—not for the love of music, but so I could have another item to put down for my college application. Neither of my parents could play an instrument. And we never sang songs in the car or listened to music on the radio. I was supposed to do math problems or read a science book during commutes. And never would my parents ever have spent money on a noisy, pointless set of drums.

Contrast this with my friend John. John's parents love music and they go dancing. John's family sings songs on road trips. For Halloween, John dressed up as a rock star. (My kids dress up as scientists or engineers...and once as ninjas.) John's parents took him to rock concerts. At weddings in John's extended family, relatives take turns singing songs to the newly married couple. John sings all the time and loves music. For John, music conjured thoughts of fun times with family and friends. For me and the Asian American friends I hung out with, music meant getting into a better college.

Now, do you suppose these different upbringings affect how individuals might sing at church?

The fact is, some cultures have group singing as a normal part of their lives. But in my Chinese American context, we never sang. So, imagine trying to lead a bunch of insecure, Chinese American middle school kids to sing songs about loving Jesus. Not all Asian Americans are this reserved. But in my experience, Chinese Americans are some of the most reserved, inhibited, and guarded singers in the Kingdom of God. I am not critiquing the Chinese heritage church. Sometimes this reservation can be helpful. For instance, Chinese Americans seem less likely to make emotional, spurious commitments at retreats and conferences. But this reservation toward singing can hinder corporate worship.

If You Really Loved Jesus, You'd Sing More

Why do I share all this? I want to help you more fully understand the situation. Sometimes worship leaders are too hard on themselves. They wonder why the congregation doesn't clap or sing louder. Maybe it's because they don't sing at all! Sometimes worship leaders think a certain congregation loves Jesus more than another congregation does. I know a worship leader who came to my church from another church. After spending some time in our church, we had this conversation.

He said, "I think people in this church are not as passionate about Jesus."

"What makes you think that?" I asked.

He said, "Because they don't get into the worship songs. They don't smile when they sing about joy. And they don't clap during songs, ever. If they really loved Jesus, they ought to show it when they sing about Jesus. My last congregation did all those things."

I smiled and said, "Yes, but this is a predominantly

Chinese American congregation. Your previous congregation was Korean American."
He said, "Oh. Right."

Culture and Expressiveness

Perhaps you found the conversation above off-putting, or even stereotypical. It may surprise you that this is a consistent conversation I have when in ministry partnerships among Chinese Americans and Korean Americans. And, as I mentioned above, it seems to fit with the observations of others, such as Erin Meyer in *The Culture Map*.

Now, it's tricky but worthwhile to figure out if a group or individual is not singing as loudly because they are inhibited, or if they simply have a different basic level of expressiveness. As an Asian American growing up in Los Angeles, and now raising Asian American children in the Boston area, I've been told many times that my kids are "in their shells" and they need to "break out of their shells."

Depending on the situation, I may thank the person who suggests this for their input and say nothing more. Other times, I may chance the opportunity to express that my sons may not be inside any "shell." They may simply be Chinese, and thus, probably less expressive than you (as a Korean or Caucasian), and you may be projecting your level of expressiveness onto them, and in fact, even measuring them accordingly.

It is problematic to project one's own cultural baselines onto other groups. When we begin to do this with regards to expressiveness in worship, we really need to be careful, humble, wise, and prayerful.

Now, if a congregation's level of expressiveness is befitting their cultural background, I don't see an issue. And while we always can be more expressive in our worship, that is not the same as saying we *should* be.

Just as different individuals from the same culture have differing personalities, so different cultures from this same world have different corporate personalities.

However, if an individual or group is not as expressive out of fear of judgment, embarrassment, or inhibition, then I think it is worth exploring the cause and how this individual or group can feel free to be more expressive if they choose to. But, really, that's more about becoming *less inhibited* than becoming *more expressive*. In my limited experience, as long as people do not feel unduly inhibited, I'm inclined to not try to tell them to be more expressive in worship.

The Bright Side

Serving in an Asian American church may present unique challenges for newly formed or growing worship teams. There are far fewer Asian Americans whose immigrant parents allow them to take guitar or drum lessons. Far fewer Asians who grew up singing in front of other people. And very few Chinese Americans who relish the idea of singing into a microphone for all to hear.

But there are some bright sides. In my experience, most Chinese Americans grow up learning music. They can read music. They can match pitch. They can keep a beat and stay in tempo. And they are willing to learn.

My friends who lead worship teams of Caucasian youth have to tell the kids to play softer, to hold back more, and not to crowd the spotlight. In my experience with Chinese American worship teams, I have to tell them to sing louder, to play more confidently, and not to be afraid of the spotlight.

As Asians in a white-dominated American culture, we're already used to the idea that most of the published authors, popular artists, and respected experts are white. And all minorities have to learn to take the helpful wisdom from these white, often middle-class believers and adapt them to our situations. Raising up worship teams is no different. Read and learn from the respected worship leaders of our day. But spend prayer and thoughtfulness adapting their helpful insights to your Asian American, small church worship team.

WORKBOOK

Chapter Seven Questions

Your Heart: What ethnic and cultural hindrances do you face when it comes to worship? What are some strengths of your ethnicity/culture? How are the strengths and weaknesses sometimes misunderstood by other groups within the white, middle-class American church at large?

_____

_____

_____

_____

_____

_____

_____

_____

_____

Your Church: Do you have to "hold back" or "urge forward" your worship team? How about your congregation? Are they comfortable with outward displays of emotion such as clapping, hand raising, swaying, etc.? How does your church's outward responsiveness affect you as a worship leader? What are some other, less visible ways to gauge the congregation's connection with worship?

_____
_____
_____
_____
_____
_____
_____
_____
_____
_____

Your Commitment: Thank God for your heritage, including its unique challenges, limitations, and strengths. Talk to a worship leader from a different culture/ethnic group about the specific challenges of your respective congregations. Purpose to regularly pray for one another in your worship ministries.

_____
_____

Chapter Seven Notes

Part Two:
Pick the Best Songs

PART TWO: PICK THE BEST SONGS

Chapter Eight:
The Song's Message

As a worship leader, you should do your best to serve your flock and exalt God. Who would disagree with that? But what does that mean exactly? To play your best music? Yes. To sing with your best voice? Agreed. To lead with your best skill? Agreed. To choose the best songs? Things get a little trickier here.

Can one really say some songs are good while others are bad? Isn't this more about preference? After all, "Beauty is in the eye of the beholder," right?

Isn't Music About Preference?

But what if beauty were *not* in the eye of the beholder? What if the standards of beauty were objective, not subjective? If there were objective standards of beauty, shouldn't we select the best songs based upon those standards?

What if there were objective standards to evaluate art? If there were, wouldn't God deserve our best? After all, our songs and music are offerings to God. The shepherd was to offer the *best* of his flock (Leviticus 9:2; Genesis 4:4). The farmer was to offer the *best* of his harvest (Deuteronomy 26:2–4, Exodus 23:19). It follows that the musician should offer the *best* of his music selection.

When looking for the best songs to offer during a worship service, I suggest considering the following three key elements: the song's message, the song's music, and the song's match. Each plays a crucial role in drawing the leader, the musician, and the congregation into a closer spirit of worship with the Lord.

The Song's Message

The first criterion of good music evaluates the *message* of the song. If the song has lyrics, then consider what message the lyrics communicate. Biblical worship should accord with biblical doctrine. Thus, we should evaluate songs for their meaning. A good song tells a biblically sound message.

Look at the song's lyrics. If the song has words, then the majority of the song's message comes through the lyrics.

Do the Lyrics Convey Biblical Truth?

Do the words correspond with the gospel of Jesus Christ? Would your pastor find the words theologically sound? Would God be pleased or honored by the words?

Conveying biblical truth is more than not saying anything wrong. It's about lyrics espousing biblical truth. Many songs don't say anything biblically incorrect, but they also don't say much biblically at all.

Examples of such songs include "In the Secret" aka "I Want to Know You" and "Draw Me Close." Take a moment and look up the lyrics. Read the lyrics and see what they say and what they don't say. There's not much wrong with these songs, though some cultures or personalities might find the terms too intimate. But there's also not much right in them either. In fact, they could be sung to a godly spouse as much as they could be sung to God!

That leads to another idea: Can this song be happily sung by other groups who are not evangelical Christians? Can this song be sung by good Jews or good Muslims (which are other monotheistic religions)? Could you lead these songs in a Jewish synagogue or a Muslim mosque? If yes, then there's nothing distinctly Christian about them. They may not contain anything inconsistent with the gospel, but they may not contain anything explicit that sets it apart as a Christian worship song.

Let's consider one example of this in the doctrine of the Trinity, especially the eternal divinity of Jesus Christ and the Holy Spirit. Hymns such as "How Great Thou Art" or "Praise to the Lord, the Almighty" or "Great Is Thy Faithfulness" and other great classics say nothing distinctly Trinitarian or Christian. Don't believe me? Go back and look at the lyrics and ask yourself if your Jehovah's Witnesses friends could sing this in their Kingdom Halls. Jehovah's Witnesses don't believe Jesus is the eternal Son of God and thus don't believe in the Trinity. Would they not adore the lyrics to "Great Is Thy Faithfulness"?

Does this mean we shouldn't sing those songs? No, not necessarily. We can continue to sing these songs because they do convey some truths. But by themselves, they don't contain the fullness of the gospel and our Triune God. Worship leaders must consider the combined messages of the songs we choose to lead.

More people get their theology from worship songs than sermons. Songwriter Rich Mullins pointed out that few remember any sermons by John Wesley.[3] But his songs are sung in churches throughout the world today. Fortunately, his rich theology permeates his songs.

At the very least, worship songs should not say anything incorrect. (And here, some will find me nit-picky.) But sometimes, they do. I love a modern hymn called "How Deep the Father's Love for Us."[4] It's my kind of song. Musically rich. Lyrically dense. I could sing songs like this all day.

But there's a subtle error, in my opinion, in the song. In the second verse, there's a line that reads:

> *It was my sin that held Him there*
> *Until it was accomplished...*

I appreciate the sentiment behind that line. I've heard many preachers proclaim, "It was our sins that held Jesus upon that cross!" But I disagree. Jesus was not compelled to die on a cross because of my sin. Rather, Jesus was compelled to die because of His obedience to the Father and His love for us.

> *For this reason the Father loves me, because I lay down my life that I may take it up again. No one takes it from me, but I lay it down of my own accord. I have authority to lay it down, and I have authority to take it up again. This charge I have received from my Father.*
> —*John 10:17–18*

The sentimentalism in the hymn smacks of reducing the glorious obedience of Christ to a mere inability to get off that cross. In my church, after a sermon on this very subject of the cross, we changed the lyrics thus:

> *It was His love that held Him there*
> *Until it was accomplished...*

Not my sin, but His love. Jesus stayed on the cross because He loves and obeys the heavenly Father. Jesus stayed on the cross because He loves us. Jesus had all the power and right to come down from the cross. What held him there was not my sin, but His love. (See also Hebrews 12:2)

God will hold worship leaders accountable for the worship songs we choose to lead in our services. We have a responsibility to choose songs that reflect the truth of God's message. So please rethink this if you find this nitpicking, or unimportant. You may differ on this particular song. That's fine. My point is that worship leaders need spiritual discernment when evaluating a song's message. Do not be frivolous and merely pick songs that sound good. Be intentional, use discernment, and ask God to give you wisdom if the songs you choose are an accurate reflection of His truth.

Are the Lyrics Well-Written?

The second feature of the song's message has to do with the style and form of the words. We should ask this: Are the lyrics well written poetry and/or prose?

You can get a sense of lyrical quality this way: Read the lyrics without the music. Read the lyrics aloud, without hearing the melody in your head, as if you didn't know the tune. Does the poetry capture your imagination? Does the prose conjure up God's beauty as best able to be captured by human language? History has preserved some of the best lines written in poetry and song.

The best lines can be simple or complex. But you usually recognize them when you see them.

Joyful, joyful we adore Thee
God of glory, Lord of love;

> *Hearts unfold like flowers before Thee,*
> *Op'ning to the sun above.*[5]

Or another song recently revived:

> *When Satan tempts me to despair*
> *And tells me of the guilt within*
> *Upward I look and see Him there*
> *Who made an end to all my sin.*[6]

Or a very recent song:

> *Who, O Lord, could save themselves*
> *Their own soul could heal?*
> *Our shame was deeper than the sea*
> *Your grace is deeper still.*[7]

Not only do I think these songs have great music. But when you read the lyrics without music, the lines possess good cadence, imagery, and rhyme. Songs don't have to rhyme, but I am partial to a well-written rhyme—at least some of the time.

I'm not saying that you shouldn't sing songs with simple lyrics. Composers labor over their lyrics. We should encourage and thank the songwriters among us. That being said, I encourage you as a worship leader to consider the quality and excellence of the lyrics for the songs you use in worship.

Some lyrics sing well but read horribly. Sometimes I love a song's lyrics the first time I sing a song. Then I go home and look up the lyrics and read them aloud to my friend who has not yet heard (or sung) the song and discover it doesn't have the same emotional resonance.

When you consider a song's lyrics by their own literary merits, you may find that sometimes it's the music that lifts the lyrics rather than the music and lyrics working together to draw the singer into a spirit of worship. We'll discuss this aspect of worship more in the next chapter.

WORKBOOK

Chapter Eight Questions

Your Heart: Describe a time when the right song at the right time impacted your walk with God more powerfully than a sermon or Bible study. What truths in that song stood out to you and why?

_____
_____
_____
_____
_____
_____
_____
_____
_____
_____

Your Church: Now ask members of your worship team and/or congregation to share a "song testimony"—how lyrics to a song instructed, encouraged, or convicted them. What type of songs do they mention? Are they songs with a strong biblical message?

_____
_____
_____
_____
_____
_____
_____
_____
_____
_____

Your Commitment: Make a list of the top fifty songs that your congregation sings or that you would like to use. Read through the lyrics of each one separate from its tune. Divide them into categories: "Poor" for any that are biblically weak or poorly written, "Fair" for songs that do convey truth but are not biblically specific enough to apply only to evangelical Christianity, "Good" for songs that are biblically strong but may have a line or two that needs revision, and "Excellent" for songs that are biblically strong with well-written and appealing lyrics.

Note: See Appendix A: Song-Categorizing Worksheet for a comprehensive way to evaluate all the aspects of a song discussed in this book.

_____
_____
_____
_____
_____
_____
_____
_____
_____
_____

Chapter Eight Notes

PART TWO: PICK THE BEST SONGS

Chapter Nine:
The Song's Music—
Honor Through Excellence

The second criterion when selecting worship songs is evaluating the song's music. After we consider the lyrical content, we should ask ourselves, "Is this song musically excellent?"

Now, I am not a professional musician, so I apologize for any musical naivete. I have, however, tested these ideas with my professional musician friends and have benefited from their input about what makes good music.

Just as there are excellent lines of words and there are terrible lines of words, there are some lines of music that are sublime while others cause the hearer to grind their teeth. When evaluating music, musicians consider a piece's meter, progression, rhythm, simplicity, and authenticity to determine what works and what doesn't.

Excellence Versus Preference

When selecting music for a worship service, it's

important to note that there is a difference between excellence and preference. Excellence deals with the overall quality of the song. Preference deals with someone's enjoyment of the song. Consider how we look at food or movies.

For food, I may taste a new dish, say, duck liver. I may be trained to appreciate the texture, the skill of the chef who prepared it, and so forth. But that doesn't mean I enjoy the taste. I may enjoy eating hot dogs more than filet mignon, but I can still recognize the excellence in a well-prepared steak.

For another food item, consider the fruit known as durian, which is a prickly fruit with a very pungent scent that is native to Southeast Asia. I may learn that a delicious, ideal durian has a specific consistency, aroma, and skin. I can appreciate a good durian prepared well, but that doesn't mean I will ever want to eat it!

Or take movies. I may dislike a certain movie, say, *Pirates of the Caribbean 4*. I can *agree* that the actors may have done a great job or that the special effects blended right in or that the musical score matched the movie and still not *enjoy* the movie. It could be that the genre is not one I prefer to watch. Or perhaps I'm just not interested in watching yet another pirate movie.

The same is true of music.

I prefer songs with more content to simple, repetitive songs. I realized this at the Lausanne Congress at Cape Town in 2010. This gathering of evangelical Christians from around the world featured diverse worship styles and teams. I remember when a worship team from Africa came up to lead. The stage was full of men and women dancing and playing tambourines. They wore bright outfits. And the song was basically one line: "We are walking in the light of God." They emphasized that by having us literally walk around the room. We stomped. We clapped. We swayed as worship leaders marched around the stage and the congregation marched around tables. It was a good time, and I appreciated it.

Later on, a worship team from Great Britain came along. The small orchestral ensemble led us to sing "In Christ Alone," a lengthy song that is filled with deep imagery and theology.

Here are my observations from that. During the high-energy, one-liner song, the Brits politely clapped. During the wordy modern-day hymn, the boisterous Africans politely sang. Each respected the various musical styles, but each preferred their own type of music.

Forgive these stereotypes, but I realized I'm more "stuffy Brit" than "boisterous African." I can sing the one-line song, but I'd prefer a rich, vivid hymn chock-full of biblical allusions, imagery, and theology. This leads to our next point.

When people say, "This song stinks," they're not usually commenting on the technical excellence of the song. They probably mean, "This song doesn't match my musical preference." Just as with my food and movie tastes, I can acknowledge that a song is musically excellent without liking the song. And vice versa. I may enjoy a song and yet admit it's technically not a good song.

My goal is to encourage worship leaders to think objectively about songs they choose for their worship sets. This requires learning to appreciate and recognize good songs. However far you have come in understanding and appreciating music, choose the best songs you can.

Judging Artistic Excellence

Francis Schaeffer gave four criteria for judging artistic excellence in his little book, *Art and the Bible*.[8] You may find them helpful.

- Technical excellence—We can praise the artist for their technical excellence even if we disagree with their worldview.
- Validity—Is the artist being true to themselves and their worldview, or are they simply making art for the money or to be accepted?
- Intellectual content, the worldview that comes through—What is the artist's worldview, and how does that compare to Scripture?
- The integration of the content and the vehicle—Does the content of the art suit the method that the artist has chosen to present the content?

Each of these criteria help us consider the artistic excellence of a piece of art. I believe you can use this to think about songs as well.

How Do We Choose Songs?

So, even if we could choose songs that are objectively more excellent, does that mean we always should? Does that mean it's somehow wrong or even a sin not to select the best songs? How do we pick the best songs while avoiding elitist snobbery?

I don't want to produce snobby worship leaders. But in a gracious and thoughtful manner, we should encourage and pursue the best for God. While we may still disagree on what songs we like or believe to be more excellent, we can show grace to another as we grow in this area of worship leadership.

WORKBOOK

Chapter Nine Questions

Your Heart: What are some of your personal preferences when it comes to style of music? What are some types or styles of music that, even if performed excellently, will likely never be your preference?

_____
_____
_____
_____
_____
_____
_____
_____
_____
_____

Your Church: Can a song be both "easy" to play and "excellent" in quality? What are some songs that are simple for untrained musicians to play/sing, but still superior in musical excellence? What are some songs that are somewhat more complex but worth the extra effort for both the worship team and congregation to master?

_____
_____
_____
_____
_____
_____
_____
_____
_____

Your Commitment: Look at the four criteria of artistic excellence as quoted from Francis Schaeffer. Evaluate the songs your team has performed in the last month based on these standards. Would you say that you are choosing excellent music? Why or why not, and what area might you need to consider more closely?

_____
_____
_____

Chapter Nine Notes

PART TWO: PICK THE BEST SONGS

Chapter Ten:
The Song's Match—
Fit the Context

We are not done yet after we have considered a song's message and a song's music. Just because a song has a biblical message and excellent music does not mean that song automatically fits into your situation.

For example, some Asian subgroups are quite expressive in worship, such as Koreans, Filipinos, and Cantonese. Other Asian subgroups tend to be less so: Chinese Americans and perhaps Japanese.

At CapeTown 2010, we saw a video of worship gatherings from different parts of the world. The African worship service had exuberant dancing, ribbons, and tambourines. The American worship service featured driving rock 'n' roll. The Chinese service showed people sitting in a circle politely singing from hymnals. I thought, "How (stereo-)typical."

I admit there are exceptions to these generalizations. And yet I have learned much about selecting worship songs to help bring out expressiveness from less expressive Asian Americans, especially first-generation

American-born Chinese

I've led worship with largely Caucasian groups and largely Korean groups and even largely African American groups. All those groups seemed far more eager to get into the music, sing out, clap, and even dance than the American-born Chinese, who are usually much less "into" the music and seem more subdued.

I say "seem" more subdued because, in my view, these folks are in fact "into" worship and the music. They just look different due to cultural differences. This is important because worship leaders may mistakenly believe that these Chinese Americans were not worshiping. I've seen worship leaders chastise or even berate some congregations for "not getting into worship" or for "not worshiping from the heart."

I can see why those worship leaders believed that the level of expressiveness implied that congregation members were not engaged in the worship. Those worship leaders were gauging the engagement level of this predominantly Chinese American congregation in the same way they would Caucasian congregations. But they did not realize the context of Chinese American spirituality and expressiveness.

It is problematic to equate outward expression with genuine worship. We should not assume that just because someone sings a song to God in tears, they actually mean what they say. In fact, I have concerns when I observe people getting into worship because they appear to be carried away by the music. (Obviously I can't read people's minds, so I can't know for sure.) I rarely have that concern with Chinese Americans, who generally seem less prone to being swept away in mere emotional expressions. However, my concern for my Chinese American brethren has been to encourage them to grow in sincere expressiveness.

Another challenge in Asian American churches is the increased cultural gap on top of the generational gap. I've served in a congregation where I had a seventy-year-old first generation immigrant Chinese American man standing in worship next to a thirteen-year-old Chinese American girl who was born in the States. Imagine their potentially divergent musical tastes.

Now imagine trying to come up with a worship set that would engage these two people with such contrasting cultural, musical, and emotional backgrounds. I hoped to encourage the teenage girl to sing hymns while encouraging the senior citizen to clap to a modern worship song.

Baseball great Ted Williams once said that the hardest thing in all professional sports was hitting a baseball traveling at 100 miles an hour.[9] Well, perhaps the hardest thing in all of worship leading is leading an inhibited, minority Chinese American congregation in New England to worship freely, expressively, and unashamedly.

Choosing the Right Songs

The third criterion of selecting a good song is asking how well a song matches a given context, such as the racial or ethnic background of your congregation. Consider these following points as additional guides as you select songs for your worship service.

Songs Should Match Your Team's Ability

Pick music you can play. Don't choose a song that fits with the sermon if your team cannot play it well. Ask yourself: Can your worship team play the song well enough? Can they play it in a way that will not distract congregation members?

Often a worship leader chooses a worship song that everyone agrees has a biblical message and great music. The worship team loves the song. The pastor loves the song. The congregation loves the song. Even the guest speaker loves the song. If everyone loves the song, why not lead it?

One reason is this: Your team can't play it well enough. What is "well enough" depends on your context. Even the musically untrained can sense when a music team is uncomfortable with a song. They'll notice if the team loses its place or struggles with the transition from the bridge to the chorus, or if the vocalists are struggling to sing on key.

If your congregation is larger and includes professional musicians or music students, the standard will be even higher. That's because any mistakes in the music will distract their trained ears. While it may be beneficial for those with trained ears to be willing and ready to give the worship team grace—we still have a responsibility to do our best to lift our standard to avoid hindering the worship of our congregation. If your congregation is smaller or has few or no professional musicians, they may be more forgiving, especially if the worship team is still new to leading.

Songs Should Match Your Congregation Lyrically

You are a servant-leader, so find songs that serve your congregation well, that are accessible for them to sing, and that direct them to God through their preferred styles. You should not thoughtlessly force a rural tribe in China to sing our modern American songs or vice versa.

For example: In my Chinese American context, I find younger generations who grew up in America more expressive when it comes to individual emotions. But the older generations, especially those who grew up overseas, are less expressive. My immigrant Chinese parents would never sing a line like "Whisper my own love song ... to You, my Dad and King."[10] Nor would they have prayed with such language. I am not saying we should cater to the whims of the congregation, but the wise servant-leader is sensitive to the congregation's unique tastes.

On the other hand, in my Chinese American context, I found older generations who grew up on hymns to sing much more loudly in general than their children, who might have grown up feeling like minorities or unaccepted by broader American Anglo culture. It all depends on your congregation.

Some churches are full of singers who sing their loudest. Other churches have musically shy singers. Know your flock. If you're not sure, ask your pastor or other leaders.

Don't pick songs soaked in emotion if the congregation isn't ready to sing those songs. Likewise, don't pick songs with lengthy, dense doctrinal statements if your congregation won't be able to keep up. If you want to stretch your congregation in any of these areas, do so prayerfully and in dialogue with your pastor and other leaders. Just remember that change takes time.

As a leader, you may wish to expand your congregation's musical horizons. However, that's secondary to serving them by selecting songs that match their tastes, expressiveness, and musical development. If your congregation is more reserved, consider beginning with songs that are more traditional in tone and voice. If it's more expressive, look for songs that allow them to engage in music that encourages them to raise their hands or move with the rhythm. As you become more comfortable with each other, you'll be able to introduce them to different styles of music as appropriate for your context.

Songs Should Match the Congregation Musically

People have different tastes in music. Would you expect a white congregation to have the same tastes as a black congregation? Would an aging church of retirees like the same music as a youth group? If people have different tastes, then the worship leader should consider this in song selection.

Your tastes as the worship leader might not be the same as the congregation's tastes. Or the pastor's tastes. So, whose tastes rule the day?

I would suggest that you defer to your pastor first and congregation second. Ask your pastor and submit to him. Understand your congregation and serve them. Your own personal musical tastes are the lowest priority. Isn't that a part of servant-leadership?

What if you have a mix of cultures or races in your congregation?

This raises a whole other topic of multicultural and multiethnic churches. But for now, I'd offer this. Be intentional about the musical styles you lead your congregation to sing. Coordinate this with your pastoral leadership. I urge you to not go out on a personal, private mission to make your congregation sing louder, faster, wordier, quieter, or whatever your personal goals are. As worship leaders, you should not have any "personal goals" but a coordinated, united sense of how the Holy Spirit wants to grow your congregation in worship.

What about your congregation? Do you know their musical styles, tastes, preferences, and quirks? If not, learn them. If you do, are you serving them well? And if you do know their current musical styles and tastes, have you entered a dialogue as to how God might want your congregation to grow or expand musically? This may require you to grow and expand your horizons of music or worship.

If you need help deciding what to play, ask a trusted worship leader. Definitely ask your pastor what he thinks about songs and arrangements. Ask him if he knows a little about music. Even if he doesn't, he knows something else just as important: He knows the congregation. He'll be able to provide insight about your congregation's response to various songs.

WORKBOOK

Chapter Ten Questions

Your Heart: Spend some time in prayer asking the Lord to search for your heart for any personal goals or agenda regarding your worship ministry. Ask for His help in setting aside these things to best follow the Holy Spirit and serve the needs of your congregation. Are there songs or styles of music that you don't personally prefer, but that would serve your church well?

_____
_____
_____
_____
_____
_____
_____
_____
_____
_____

Your Church: Ask members of your congregation to tell you their favorite hymns or worship songs. Look for themes as far as which songs resonate with your people and why that might be. Are certain songs more popular with different age groups or "subcultures" within the church?

How would you describe your congregation's musical tastes/preferences?

- Fast, slow, or medium tempo?
- Upbeat/joyful or quiet/contemplative?
- Lots of words or fewer words?
- What musical genres helps them express their worship well?
- What musical genres seem not to work for them at this time?

_____
_____
_____
_____
_____
_____
_____
_____
_____

Your Commitment: Plan a time to talk extensively with your pastor about his goals for congregational worship. Are there certain songs or styles that he is uncomfortable with? What observations has he made about the congregation and the type of worship that works most effectively for them? (You may want to read Chapter Thirty on "Pastors Versus Worship Leaders" as well as "A Note for the Pastor" prior to this discussion.

Chapter Ten Notes

Part Three:
Sets

PART THREE: SETS

Chapter Eleven: Start with a Theme, Mood, or Song

Now that we've talked about what your worship team looks like and decided on what type of music suits your setting the best, it's time to talk about planning worship sets. In the next few chapters, I present different principles on how to how to select, order, and arrange songs. I list these principles in a basic order so that you can learn each concept in a step-by-step fashion. Once you become more aware of these concepts, you'll be able to apply these methods in the manner that works best for you.

I generally pick one of three starting points when planning a worship set: a theme, a mood, or a song.

Planning a Theme-Based Worship Set

By "theme," I mean a common idea that connects a particular set of songs, such as the theme of a sermon (i.e., sharing the gospel), the theme of the season (i.e., Christmas or Easter), or the theme of the circumstances (i.e., a funeral or national remembrance).

When I want the worship set to align with the sermon, I coordinate with the pastor or speaker. I ask if there are any particular ideas or themes he or she has in mind for the music. I'll ask the speaker to provide as much sermon information as possible and to indicate whether there is a specific song he or she would like included in the worship.

I do this to serve and support my pastor or the speaker. But I don't promise I can do everything he or she asks. I may not know the song, or I may think the song is musically inappropriate. But I will do my best to work with the pastor.

Why should the music and message match thematically? Imagine a worship service where the theme of the music did not match the theme of the message. For example, the pastor is teaching about loving your neighbor, but the music is about God being triumphant. I suppose there's nothing wrong with such a service, but wouldn't it be better to have worship that fits with the sermon and vice versa?

This is especially true for songs that follow the sermon. Following the same sermon example, imagine the Holy Spirit has convicted the congregation of the necessity for Christians to love others. People feel stirred up. They're thinking, "Yes, we really need to love our neighbors more!" Then, after this convicting sermon, the worship leader invites the congregation to respond by singing "It Is Well with My Soul," which is about God's peace amidst trials. You might as well be giving your church emotional or spiritual whiplash!

As worship leaders, we must be thoughtful about these worship elements. Such practice seems to fail to honor what the Spirit is doing in the hearts of the people. We should align our songs with how the Spirit is moving.

This does not mean that the purpose of the music is to prepare people for the sermon. Worship happens both in the music and the message. But in practice, the pastor sets the preaching plan, so it makes sense that the worship songs align with the preaching so that there is unity in the worship.

Besides the sermon, I also pick worship songs based upon the theme of the season. In more liturgical churches, you can pick the worship songs based upon the church calendar, such as the season of Advent, Lent, etc.

You can also pick songs based upon regional seasons. Do African American churches sing songs appropriate for Martin Luther King Jr's birthday? Do American churches sing about being thankful during November? Consider these as you plan a worship set.

There are some who might object to this. Should we really select our worship themes based upon contrived human holidays like Mother's Day, Labor Day, or Independence Day? I suggest that you go back to the first theme source: the sermon. If your pastor doesn't give much attention to Father's Day, then you probably should match your songs to whatever he's going to preach on. But if your pastor planned a Father's Day sermon on the fatherhood of God, then songs that focus on fatherhood or God the Father would be appropriate.

A third theme consideration is the circumstances in the life of your church. Some circumstances have the potential to capture the attention of your entire congregation. Some of those circumstances are good; some are bad.

Major events can affect your theme. Consider how you would pick songs differently in these circumstances: the death of a young child in the church, a church member hospitalized in critical condition from a freak accident, a youth missions' team being sent out, or the anniversary of September 11.

In such times, you know your people are preoccupied. Serve them by directing their attention to God and reminding them of His presence in the midst of the life-changing things we experience.

Planning a Mood-Based Worship Set

By "mood," I mean the general emotion or feeling that you want to express in worship. Different songs convey different moods. Some songs, like "Joyful, Joyful, We Adore Thee," inspire hope and lift the spirit. Other songs, like "When I Survey the Wondrous Cross," make one contemplative and reflective. If you've never considered song moods, this will give you a new way of categorizing songs.

When I suggest that you start picking songs based upon the mood, consider the appropriate mood of the service. Is the service a celebration, like a church anniversary or dedicating a new building? Then pick uplifting songs. If the service is somber, like a funeral or a Good Friday service, then select the songs that are more reflective.

I also suggest that you focus on only one theme or mood. Most people cannot bounce between totally different emotions in the same worship set. Again, we want to avoid emotional whiplash. Determining what attribute of God, what response to God, or what theme or mood your songs and music will address in advance will allow you to best select the songs for your mood-based worship sets. Ask yourself if you want people to respond to God with thanksgiving or with humility. Are you trying to express repentance for sin or boldness for evangelism? Remember, whatever song you pick will guide people's moods and will play a role in how they respond to the message that's been prepared.

As an aside, sometimes people are afraid of manipulating people's emotions through song selection. That's a legitimate concern, but that doesn't make selecting songs with a specific mood in mind wrong. Music, by its very nature, stirs emotions. Every song will arouse a particular emotion, so we might as well plan accordingly.

In fact, worship leaders who don't consider moods may find they are projecting their own moods into the worship sets. If the worship leader is having a good week, then he will pick happy songs. If the worship leader has been having a rough week, then he may pick hopeful songs. While a worship leader should consider his current state of mind, he should select a set mood for reasons besides just his own life situation.

Planning a Song-Based Worship Set

Perhaps you don't have a strong direction in terms of a theme or a mood for your worship set. At the very least, you can pick a song to set the tone for your set.

There are times when something or someone else compels us to include a particular song in our set. Perhaps most common is when the preacher for that gathering specifically requests a specific song, or if not the specific song, then a song along the lines of a particular topic.

Other times, the season compels us to pick a song. Christmas may not only compel us to select songs along a particular theme—such as the birth of Christ—it may compel us to pick specific songs, like the congregations' most beloved Christmas hymn.

There are times when I start forming a worship set because there's a song I really want to include. Maybe I just learned the song, and I really like it. Maybe a fellow worship leader taught the song last week and I want to reinforce this new song.

Maybe my team has practiced this song and they love playing it. Maybe I believe this song fits with the Scripture this week.

The point is, sometimes we don't have a clear idea of a proper theme or mood for the set. We just know we want to include a particular song. If the song fits all the basic requirements for your worship service, then go for it.

Song Selection

Once you have your theme, mood, or anchor song selected, start picking songs that fit. Keep selecting songs until you have a list with enough songs for you to choose from. The length of the list depends on how many songs will be in the final set; if you have a few extra you can't use, you can always set them aside for another week with a similar theme or mood.

Now that you have your list, you can pare it down using the song criteria in previous chapters. From there you will need to order them in the set, which we'll cover in the next few chapters.

WORKBOOK

Chapter Eleven Questions

Your Heart: If you have planned worship sets before, how do you typically come up with your songs? Do you find that you tend to base a worship set on a theme, a mood, a song, or something else? What is a song that would make a strong anchor song for a worship set when there is no clear theme needed?

_____
_____
_____
_____
_____
_____
_____
_____

Your Church: Does your pastor plan sermon series in advance? What preaching themes is he sensing God's leadership toward in the coming months? How can you be preparing for these themes?

_____
_____
_____
_____
_____
_____
_____
_____
_____
_____

Your Commitment: List out seasonal themes and circumstantial themes that will or likely will come up in the course of a year. What mood should the music for each of these sets convey? Looking over your list, are there any gaps in your music that need to be filled soon?

_____
_____
_____
_____

Chapter Eleven Notes

PART THREE: SETS

Chapter Twelve:
Think Movements, Not Songs

When you look at a worship set list of songs, what do you see? Do you see a bunch of individual songs? Or do you see something else? I don't just see individual songs, I see movements.

Let's say a worship set has six songs. You can think of this set as a list of six individual songs. But instead of individual songs, I suggest you think of them as *groups of songs* in the set. I call these groups of songs "movements." From this we can now form a definition for a worship set:

- a movement is a group of songs
- a worship set is comprised of multiple movements

We can visualize the difference between individual songs and movements in the following chart. For our example, let's consider each movement as made up of two songs. That means this set has three movements.

Worship Set of Individual Songs	Worship Set of Multiple Movements
Song 1￼Song 2￼Song 3￼Song 4￼Song 5￼Song 6	*Movement 1*￼Song 1￼Song 2￼*Movement 2*￼Song 3￼Song 4￼*Movement 3*￼Song 5￼Song 6

Next, we group the songs into movements. Think of it like pairing certain items of clothing together. Some shirts go better with certain pairs of pants than others. At least that's what my wife tells me almost every morning. In the same way, I believe some songs go better together and others don't mix well at all.

So, how do we pick what songs go together in the same movement?

Songs That Go Well Together

There are different reasons songs go well together. A group of songs might go well together because of similar themes or images. Or perhaps they share similar chord progression or rhythm. Or maybe they convey a similar mood or emotion.

By the way, just because song titles have a word in common, that doesn't mean the songs go together well. You should read through all the lyrics of the song.

Songs may go together because they effectively transition the dynamics of the set. Some slower songs tend to build toward faster songs, and vice versa.

Sometimes worship leaders group songs into a

movement because they are in the same key. I wouldn't recommend this as a primary reason to group songs. Since you can play a song in any key, technically all songs can be in the same key. Just because two songs were recorded in the same key doesn't mean they fit thematically, lyrically, or emotionally.

Finding songs that go well together involves musical skill, practice, and experience. Ask for feedback from your worship team, your pastor, and your congregation members. In time, you'll begin to see what songs work well together and for your particular context.

To recap, songs might go well together based upon these features:

- Similar themes (justice, mercy, holiness, etc.)
- Similar mood (upbeat, reflective, pleading with God, etc.)
- Similar rhythm
- Similar chord progression
- Good transition from slow to fast (and vice versa)

Make Your Movements

When learning to create movements, I suggest experimenting with different song groupings. Try playing different songs one after another. Listen for how songs dynamically flow into one another, then put your songs into movements based on what sounds best.

After you have grouped your songs into movements, the next step is to order your movements. In our example of six songs, you have three movements of two songs each. This may vary for you based on time and setting.

Exercise: Pairing Songs

Try this exercise to help develop an ear for what songs go well together. You can do this exercise on your own or as a worship team.

- Pick a worship song—any worship song.
- Now pick another five worship songs at random.
- From this list of five candidates, figure out which songs fit well with the first song.
- Ask: Do any of the five songs have a similar theme or mood with the first song?
- Play each candidate song with the main song. Do any songs have similar rhythm or chord progression as the main song?
- Do any songs flow better with the main song?
- Do any of the five songs go well before or after the primary song as a transition to a different mood, movement, or theme?

If working with your team, discuss what songs seem to go well together and what don't. And discuss *why* you think so.

Practicing this exercise will help you develop an ear for arranging your sets with the best movements available. A worship set with movements that flow well does wonders for helping the congregation focus on and connect with God without distraction. But it takes practice and intentionality to develop this necessary skill as a worship leader. Invest the time needed so you can create worship sets that add to rather than take away from the service.

WORKBOOK

Chapter Twelve Questions

Your Heart: Do you typically think in terms of individual songs or do you think of movements and sets? With which movement type are you strongest: thematic, mood, rhythm, chord progression, or good transition? With which are you weakest and how can you develop in your creation of this movement?

_____

_____

_____

_____

_____

_____

_____

_____

_____

Your Church: How will having a better flow from one song to the next enhance your congregation's worship experience? How can you build on the truths of one song with a song that reinforces the same theme?

_____
_____
_____
_____
_____
_____
_____
_____
_____
_____

Your Commitment: Complete the exercise described at the end of this chapter to work on creating musical movements.

_____
_____
_____
_____
_____
_____

Chapter Twelve Notes

PART THREE: SETS

Chapter Thirteen:
Set Flow—
Planning the Dynamics

Each song has a specific energy level or mood to it. Some are upbeat, and some are somber in nature. This energy level shouldn't be confused with the tempo of the song. For example, there are slow-tempo songs that bring the singer up and fast-tempo songs that can bring a singer down, based on the words or the arrangement of the song. I refer to these upbeat songs as "Fast" and the downbeat songs as "Slow" in the rest of this chapter.

There are other ways a song can be dynamically slow or fast, but let's consider these three elements: the topic, the music, and the arrangement of the song.

Regardless of tempo, a song's topic immediately makes the song feel slow or fast. For example, songs about repentance, humility, suffering, and the crucifixion tend to feel slower, less energetic, and more contemplative. But songs about God's majesty and glory, thanksgiving, and the resurrection tend to feel more uplifting, energetic, and triumphant.

The topic also determines the lyrics. If the topic is

somber, then the lyrics will follow. That's why songs about the suffering of Christ on the cross tend to be slower in tempo and energy. This leads to the next way a song can feel slow or fast.

The music usually matches the message. Like the example above, if the key the music is played in is melancholy or contemplative, it's unlikely that the topic will be something triumphant and full of hope, such as the resurrection of Christ.

A third feature that determines song dynamics is the arrangement of the song. Some songs have more flexibility when it comes to energy. You can slow a song down by decreasing tempo, by playing fewer instruments, or by playing the instruments in a more subtle, gentle way.

You can also give more energy to a song by increasing the tempo, by using driving guitar rhythms, or by arranging powerful vocals. You can throw in a key change. You can unleash all the instruments at full volume. You get the picture.

Bottom line: Musicians can play the same song in different ways and thus create completely different arrangements with varying energy levels.

Plan the Dynamics of a Song

A song has dynamics from the beginning to end. It may start out soft and progress to loud, or vice versa. Or it may start out contemplative but end jubilant. When planning a worship set, you should plan the dynamics for the entire song—each verse, pre-chorus, stanza, or chorus. For example, consider a hymn with four verses. Verse one may start at a normal volume. Verse two gets louder. Verse three quiets down. Verse four is loudest to end strong.

Common Dynamic Plan for 4-Verse Hymn
Verse 1—normal volume
Verse 2—growing louder
Verse 3—softer
Verse 4—loudest

You could take this dynamic plan and apply it to a song with modern structure. For example, consider a song with these parts: Verse 1, Verse 2, Chorus, and Bridge.

Verse 1 and the chorus may start out at a normal volume. Verse 2 gets bigger. The chorus gets louder. The bridge quiets down. And the final time through the chorus, nothing is held back.

Common Dynamic Plan for Song
Verse 1 and chorus (1st time)—normal volume
Verse 2 and chorus (2nd time)—growing louder
Bridge—getting even louder
Chorus (3rd time)—softer, but builds up to…
Chorus (final time)—loudest

The "Power Song"

While on the topic of song dynamics, I should mention a special type of song—the so-called power song.

Some songs may appear slow when you first consider the tempo or the topic. But these songs build up energy and momentum as the song progresses. Truly, they are rightly called anthems.

During the Eighties and Nineties, anthems were songs like "Salvation Belongs to Our God" or "Shine, Jesus, Shine" or "Hail to the King." More recent anthems are songs like "Majesty" (by Delirious) or "How Great Is Our God" (by Chris Tomlin).

Power songs have a varying level of tempo, but the

lyrics and music of such songs are so powerful (hence the name "power songs") that they have the highest dynamic level of the entire set.

I used to joke with our worship leaders that you couldn't lead another song after a power song. Why? Because people were so spent after such exhilaration that singing another song would feel anticlimactic (although I do believe that one can skillfully lead another song after a power song to "bring the congregation back down" from the third heaven). We also joked about leading sets entirely comprised of power songs to exhaust our congregation. Imagine a set with the following songs:

"Did You Feel the Mountains Tremble?" (Delirious)
"The Stand" (Hillsong)
"Son of God" (Starfield)
"I Stand in Awe of You" (Hosanna Integrity)
"Shout to the Lord" (Hillsong)

Power songs aren't limited to current releases, however. There are older hymns that are just as deserving of the label "power songs" as anything written today. The hymnal version of a power set might look like this:

"Great Is Thy Faithfulness"
"Holy, Holy, Holy!"
"Crown Him with Many Crowns"
"Amazing Grace"

In both sets, each song reaches to the height of musical energy. It would be awesome to sing a set like this. Awesome and exhausting. (Especially for my context. Remember? Mostly Chinese American, socially shy, emotionally inhibited, minority-minded folks in staid New England.)

Now that we understand "slow" and "fast" songs, we

can see how these types of songs work in the overall creation of a worship set.

Set Flow Dynamics

A worship set flow falls into three basic forms. First, a set can simply be either all fast songs or all slow songs. Second, a set can move from one type of song to the other. For example, the songs can progress from "fast" to "slow" or from "slow" to "fast." Third, a worship set can have an A-B-A progression. This is a set in which the opening and closing songs are either fast or slow, with a segment of the set in the middle being the other type of song. All other flows are variations of these basic flows.

Set Flows

Same Type	Two Types	Three Types
Fast-Fast-Fast or Slow-Slow-Slow	Slow-Fast or Fast-Slow	Slow-Fast-Slow or Fast-Slow-Fast

Let's put these examples into context. Some worship sets have only fast, high-energy, upbeat songs. Some worship sets contain only slow, contemplative songs. Other worship sets start fast and go slow.

In the Eighties and Nineties, this seemed the unwritten formula for worship sets. You would always start with one or two fast songs. And then go with a medium song or two. But the last song of the set would always be a slow song. In fact, this got so predictable and forced at times, I felt it almost made congregations go through a contrived emotional journey rather than truly worshiping God.

Plan the Dynamics of a Worship Set

Just as you plan the dynamics of a song, *so should you plan the dynamics of a set*. Within one hymn, you should play each verse according to a plan. Likewise, within one set, play each song according to a plan. Play the starting movement of a set differently than the ending movement of a set.

I've seen some worship leaders follow the same dynamics for a song for five or six songs in a row. The music and words may differ, but each song is played the same. This play style becomes forced and predictable, and you risk your congregation tuning out.

Just as you plan the dynamics of a single song, the movements of the set should progress toward climax and resolution both musically and thematically.

Order the Movements

Once you have the dynamics of a worship set established, you can move on to arranging your movements. Using our previous example of a three-movement set, one movement will go at the beginning of the set, one at the middle, and one at the end. For each movement we ask this question: "Where does this movement work best? At the beginning, middle, or end of the set?" You'll want to consider the overall setup of your service. Do you welcome people into the sanctuary with singing? Do you stop for prayer and announcements? Do you have a separate offertory piece when passing the offering plate? Do you sing after the sermon concludes?

Dynamic Plan for Set
Movement 1—Call to Worship   Song 1—normal energy   Song 2—increasing energy   *Movement 2—Call to Giving*   Song 3—lower energy   Song 4—increasing energy   *Movement 3—Call to Action*   Song 5—highest energy   Song 6—descending energy (bring the congregation back down)

Arranging Songs

Once you know the order of your service and have set up your movements, you can then move on to arranging your songs. There are a few things that you should keep in mind while arranging your worship set: The songs should be songs your team members are comfortable playing and singing, and the songs should reflect the instruments you have available to you.

1. Choose song arrangements that your team can play well. This seems obvious, but leaders often neglect this. I have walked into rehearsals and found teams trying to play like a song just like the recording. That's fine if you have the skills. But if not, just play it as well you can.

If your guitar player cannot do the same intro riffs like in the YouTube video, then skip it. Or have the keyboard play it. If your drummer can't mimic the complex groove off the album, then work out a back beat that the drummer can perform. Better to play a simple arrangement well then to play a sophisticated arrangement poorly and distract worshipers.

2. Choose a key that your group can sing. When you buy worship music, look for versions with multiple keys.

Often recordings are sold in key of the recording artist, which can be too high or too low for singers who have no professional voice training. You may want to take advantage of software that can modulate keys for you for any song in the database. Pick a key that falls within the comfortable range of your group. If you lead worship in a service with adults, pick a key both men and women can sing. Remember to adjust the key if you lead worship for the children.

3. *Choose a tempo and rhythm that your team can play well and without distraction.* If a song's tempo is too difficult for a member of the band, then either have that player step out or adjust the tempo to one that allows them to play confidently.

4. *Choose music for the instruments in your band.* Some songs require a certain instrument to sound right. If you have drums, then pick songs that call for drums. If you don't have drums, then don't pick such songs. If you have a bassist, you can rely on the bass to support the sound. Otherwise, don't pick songs that rely on heavy bass.

On Sundays when I had my keyboardist, I would choose arrangements that leveraged the keyboard or piano. In fact, I would choose songs specifically because I had a particular pianist. When I had a full drum kit on the team, I would arrange songs for a big sound. But when I had only hand percussion, I would pick songs that used the beat for rhythm only.

Too often, worship leaders pick songs before they consider the skill, instrumentation, and musical style of the team or congregation. But since they've already chosen the songs, they try their best to make the team play those songs. You won't get yourself into that if you plan and arrange the worship set with these principles in mind.

Now that you've seen examples set flow and dynamics, you can analyze worship sets in your church to see how you can best improve your musical worship.

WORKBOOK

Chapter Thirteen Questions

Your Heart: Do you typically use the same dynamics and order of movements, or do you change things up regularly? Define your normal (perhaps unconscious) patterns of movements and song tempo/dynamics so that you can see ways to improve the variety and flow of your worship service.

_____

_____

_____

_____

_____

_____

_____

_____

_____

Your Church: List keys, tempo, and rhythms that work well for your singers and musicians. What instruments do you have available and are they available every week or only certain times? How can you best utilize what you currently have?

_____

_____

_____

_____

_____

_____

_____

_____

_____

_____

Your Commitment: Identify arrangements of songs that your team can play well. What are the dynamics for each individual song? Then begin to put these songs together as movements and sets. What will be the dynamics for each worship set?
Note: See Appendix B for a helpful set assessment checklist.

_____

_____

_____

Chapter Thirteen Notes

PART THREE: SETS

Chapter Fourteen:
Two Kinds of Songs—
Focusing and Expressing

Scripture teaches we should tell the truth to one another. If so, then shouldn't we tell the truth to God? You shouldn't tell someone "I love you" if you don't mean it, yet how many times in worship have we sung "I love You" to God and not meant it deep in our hearts?
What is worse: lying to one another or lying to God?
Words are empty when they lack sincerity. In the same way, true worship must be sincere. That means we truly feel and believe the words we say and sing to God.
If you lead a congregation to sing "I Love You, Lord," then you are leading them to make a claim to God. While you can't know what is in the heart of your congregation—nor are you responsible for the position of their hearts—you are accountable for the sincerity of your own heart. You can lead others in sincere worship by exemplifying it and also inviting them to contemplate their own stance before God.
So, how do worship leaders encourage sincere worship? We do this by recognizing different types of songs.

Songs That Focus Versus Songs That Express

I divide worship songs along a spectrum I call "focusing versus expressing." On one end of the spectrum are songs that serve to draw our focus away from our circumstances and distractions and redirect our attention on God. These songs can engage people regardless of what emotions or experiences they're going through.

At the other end of the spectrum are songs that encourage expressions of emotions or feelings. Inherent in an expressing song is the idea that to sing this song sincerely, you must feel what the song says you feel.

How can you tell if a song is more a focusing song or an expressing song? Ask this question: Do the lyrics claim factual statements about God or express sentiments about Him?

The words "God, You are holy" declare a statement of fact. This statement is true or false *regardless* of what we think. But the words "God, You are lovely to me" express a sentiment. The statement is true depending on *who says it*. If someone believes God is lovely, then he can express this sentiment sincerely. If someone does not believe God is lovely, he would not be sincere in saying this.

Let's take another example. Anybody can sing the words "The Lord reigns." It's true no matter who says it. But not everybody can sincerely sing, "Lord, reign in me." Why not? Because some don't believe in God. Or if they do, they don't want God to reign in their lives.

Some songs can make statements of fact or express sentiments and feelings. Some songs do both. That is why it is important that we as leaders evaluate the words of the songs we select, so we have a better understanding of what we are leading our congregation in singing.

Facts First, Then Feelings

How does knowing if a song is one that encourages focus or expression help worship leaders lead their congregation in sincere worship? This helps because *feelings follow facts*. Our emotions follow our beliefs. Thus, we encourage sincere worship when worshipers express feelings *after* they believe the facts about God.

This is a biblical model. The truth of God apprehends the soul first. After we grasp the truth of God, we respond with appropriate feelings. 1 John 4:19 states that we love because God first loved us. Our feeling (we love God) follows the fact (God first loved us).

In a worship service, that means that we lead songs that express feelings only after people can express those sentiments with sincerity. First sing songs of facts. Then sing songs of feelings.

First, focus people's attention in worship through songs about the truth of God. Then lead songs of feelings so they can express their sincere emotions and praise to God. The Holy Spirit can use songs that make us meditate on the truths of God to stir our hearts to sing our feelings to God or convict us to remain silent and consider why we don't feel the same emotions being conveyed in the song.

Let's apply this in a typical Sunday worship service. Say a worship set begins with an emotional song of gratitude to God. This song expresses a sentiment. We should therefore ask: Are people ready to sincerely express this sentiment to God?

Consider the circumstances of most people. It's early Sunday morning. Perhaps people were late in coming to church. They are rushed. They attempt to herd their children. They may have struggled to find parking. And that's just what happened that morning. What about people who had a late-night partying or studying? What about people who come to church burdened with worries over finances, jobs, and health?

In light of all this, how many people are immediately ready to sincerely sing of gratitude to God? Relatively few, I think. Yes, the song may be well written and well led. And the power of the Spirit can stir hearts to worship. But in general, we should plan our worship set to better direct people to God by selecting an opening worship song to focus people spiritually, musically, and emotionally to worship God.

Turn Their Eyes upon Jesus

Consider the different attendees to a Sunday service for whom you lead worship. One person comes to church eager to worship God. Another person comes to church out of guilt or routine. And still another person arrives at church questioning God's goodness or existence because of some type of suffering they're facing.

If you just came from the hospital bedside of your spouse, would you be ready to sing of God's goodness? Theoretically, perhaps. But most of us need reminders that God is good.

If you just lost your job, would you be ready to sing of God's faithfulness? Ideally, yes. Christians should declare God's faithfulness in the midst of trials. But in practice, most of us could use gentle and encouraging reminders that God is able to provide.

If you struggling with guilt over sexual impurity or marital unfaithfulness, would you be ready to sing of God's steadfast love and forgiveness? I would hope so, but many of us need reminders that God's mercy covers the truly repentant sinner.

If every person in our worship services were perfectly focused on God and immediately prepared to worship Him, then worship leaders would not need bother with directing people's attention away from themselves and (back) to God. But because people are not already focused, the worship leader must shepherd all these different people into the presence of God through skillful and thoughtful planning.

You are their worship leader. God has called you to serve each of these individuals and direct their attention to Him. Certain songs will help you do that more, while other songs will only make things worse. Songs about God can orient people to who God is and what He has done. Songs that convey emotion provide opportunities to express emotional praise to God.

If someone comes to church ready to worship the Lord, then starting with a song that says "I love You, God" would fit that person. But what if a person arrives struggling with believing that God cares? Such a person will not engage a song that says, "I love You, God." Instead, that person may need to sing a song that says, "God is love." After such a reminder, this person may then come again to the place where he can sincerely sing "I love You, God."

The Reason Worship Leaders Start with Feelings

The reason many worship leaders, public prayers, and pastors start with feelings in a service is because they already experienced the facts earlier. Think about it. The typical worship leader has been preparing during the week for worship. He may have spent the week engrossed in Scripture, poring over worship songs, and now he comes ready and expectant to sing to God. The worship leader started with the facts of God's glorious truth during the week. So now on Sunday, he's ready to worship. But is that true of the other people gathered?

It's important to remember that even though you, the worship leader, are ready to respond to God, your congregation may not be. They did not prepare by meditating on

Scripture. They did not wake up early to pray for the worship service. Give your congregation the gift of preparation. Provide them with an opportunity to turn their collective attention to God. Give them songs to dwell upon God's holiness, loveliness, or another of His attributes first.

Then, after they have considered God, give them songs to sing in response to God.

God as Subject and Object of Worship

To put it another way, start a set with songs in which God is the subject of the songs: "God is…" or "Great is the Lord." These songs can be sung truthfully by anyone, including someone who may not profess faith in Christ. Statements like "God loves me" or "God is compassionate" are true even if not everyone believes them. As people praise God as the *subject* of songs, they begin to focus on Him and respond to Him in His truth.

As people respond to who God is, then God becomes the *object* of our songs. Instead of singing "Blessed be the Lord" we now sing "We will bless the Lord." Instead of singing "How lovely is *Your* dwelling place, O Lord," we now sing "*My* soul longs for the Lord."

In these songs, God is no longer the subject; the singer is the subject. That follows a pattern in Psalms where the worshiper is the subject who sings to God, the object of worship.

In the debate over hymns versus modern praise songs, proponents of hymns used to make this argument. They preferred older hymns because those songs were about God (You, Thee). But newer songs were about us (I, me). Songs should be about God and not us, folks would say. That sounded really good to me, until I realized that many older hymns contained lines like "I will enter His gates" or "And when I think, that God His Son not sparing" or even "I sing the mighty power of God."

In those songs, the singer is the subject and God is the object. Thus, this argument does not hold true for many of the cherished hymns we've received from the ages. It also doesn't fit with Scripture. The Psalms contain phrases like "I will sing of steadfast love and justice; to you, O LORD I will make music" (Psalm 101:1), or "I will sing to the LORD as long as I live; I will sing praise to my God while I have being" (Psalm 104:33).

Biblical worship songs include God both as the subject, "God, You are...," and God as the object, "God, I want to..."

I suggest that worship sets progress from God as subject to God as object. After that, you can go to either song form. This is a general principle, but one that I almost always follow. This will encourage sincere worship, which, theologically is a response to God—who He is, and what He has done.

When to Start with Feeling?

Is it ever appropriate to start a worship set with emotions, expression, and sentiments? I believe so. Here are some situations that might call for an emotional approach.

After Common Experiences

When a congregation shares a common experience, they may share a similar mental state or focus on God. Such experiences include events such as a sermon or a testimony, or while at a conference or retreat. In those cases, when people have a shared experience, they are probably having a shared mental or emotional state.

Let's consider the song of response after a sermon. You can make a reasonable guess as to what people were just thinking about. Hopefully, they were thinking about the topic of the sermon! For example, let's say a sermon on repentance seemed to connect with the congregation. Then most people would be ready to sing about repentance with sincerity. Or, if we just heard a powerful sermon on the grace of God, people will be ready to sing a song in response to God's grace.

Another common experience people share would be worship at special services such as weddings or funerals. It's likely that most people are happy for the couple at a wedding. Likewise, most people attend a funeral to show respect and sympathy. In these cases, it's not as likely you'll need to help people focus since they already came prepared.

To Aspire to Sincerity

Another time to lead songs of expression before people are ready to sing sincerely is to train people toward whatever the song expresses. That is, we sing "God is faithful" not because we believe at that moment, but because we aspire to sincerely express that eventually. We sing such songs *to aspire*.

Here's a common example of how people do this. We tell children to say "sorry" when they wrong another. But when children say sorry, they don't always mean it. Often, they are not sorry. But we still make them apologize. Why? Because we hope that by practicing apologizing when they're in the wrong, they will come to mean it eventually. Likewise, I believe a leader can urge people to say things to God in the hope that the Holy Spirit will change a person's heart to eventually mean it.

If you try that, help your congregation grow into whatever aspiration you're guiding them toward. For example, I might say something like, "You may not be able to sing the lines of this song right now. But you can sing it as a prayer to God and ask him to let it be true of you."

In my experience, worship leaders do not spend enough time considering sincerity in worship. Instead, they have people sing songs the congregation neither means nor feels at the time. When worship leaders do that, we heap judgment upon ourselves for misguided worship leadership. We also heap judgment upon those we lead because they are insincere with God.

"But This Doesn't Sound Very Spiritual!"

I know it doesn't *sound* very spiritual, all this talk about facts and feelings, statements and sentiments. But what's not spiritual about it? We love because God first loved us. We forgive others even as God has, in Christ, forgiven us (Ephesians 4:32). God sought after us, yet no one seeks God. The biblical dynamic of our relationships with God is this: God initiates, we respond. The same is true with worship. Let us consider God as the subject first.

God is the first subject because we are the first object. God initiated first. God acted first on us, the objects. He created us. He offered us forgiveness. In response, we give God worship.

When we say we love God, it's after we see He first loved us. When we praise God's majesty, it's after we understand the Lord is above all. And so forth. To presume that we praise God before God reveals Himself smacks of hubris. God is. We respond. That's how it works in life, and that's how it should work in worship.

When we as leaders learn to use different types of songs and begin to recognize their dynamics and operations, we are better equipped to assist our brothers and sisters in Christ as they grow in their personal walk the Lord.

May God be pleased with worship that grows ever more sincere.

WORKBOOK

Chapter Fourteen Questions

Your Heart: Describe a time that you sang a worship song because it was required, but which made you feel insincere or hypocritical. How do you typically prepare your own heart for expressive worship?

_____
_____
_____
_____
_____
_____
_____
_____
_____
_____

Your Church: What are some of the needs and distractions that weigh on your church members as they gather for worship? What are some *focusing* songs that would help them to focus on God and prepare for more expressive worship?

_____

_____

_____

_____

_____

_____

_____

_____

_____

Your Commitment: Purpose to take ownership of leading your people in worship—that is, as much as possible, not manipulating emotions or leading your congregation to sing songs that are insincere or contrived but helping them prepare their hearts so that worship can be a natural responsive expression of their hearts.

_____

_____

_____

Chapter Fourteen Notes

PART THREE: SETS

Chapter Fifteen:
Creating Balance in a Single Set

If you pick out four good worship songs and put them together, do you automatically get a good worship set? Not necessarily. Just because you put nine good baseball players together does not mean you get a good team. You don't want nine good pitchers! To form a good team, you need different types of good players. The same is true when planning worship. You need to balance the songs in the set.

We will address two types of balance in worship sets: familiarity and diversity. But before we begin, you should always remember to balance the songs *within a particular worship set* and *over all your worship sets* for a particular congregation.

Balance Familiar Songs with Unfamiliar Songs

This does not mean including an equal number of unfamiliar and familiar songs in your worship. For every new or unfamiliar song, you should have several familiar songs, depending on your congregation. Some congregations love to learn new songs. Other congregations appreciate songs they already know. If you include a brand-new song in a set, then I suggest you use familiar songs for the rest of the set.

Why is this important? Because worship is a time to praise God, not learn a bunch of new songs. It's more appropriate to allow the worshipers the benefit of singing songs they know than to use the entire time of corporate worship for learning new songs.

When people learn a song, they focus on the music and words of the song. That means they are not focused on God. Worship should help people focus on God, thus using more familiar songs.

Another reason this is important is because people learn songs differently. Some find it easy to learn a song. They may learn the tune with just one run-through. Others take longer to learn songs. I have a friend who doesn't feel familiar with a song until he has sung it a dozen times. If I led that song every week, it would take my friend three months to learn the song. But I don't pick the same songs every week, so my friend usually finds he needs at least six months before he can sing the song with familiarity. But after six months, the people who learn songs more quickly tell me they want to learn another new song! In fact, they've grown tired of the song just when my other friend finally feels comfortable with it.

Yes, the Bible calls us to sing to the Lord a new song (Psalm 96:1 NIV). But that should be tempered with the understanding that the worship leader is there to serve the congregation in providing appropriate music and an inviting environment to sing God's praises. By providing a good ratio of old and new songs, we do just that.

We should also keep in mind that nonbelievers could be present, or we may have visitors from other churches who may not know the same songs. I once attended a

Christian conference where the worship leader led each song only once over the entire weekend. Most of the Christians knew the songs, so they didn't mind. In fact, many of them enjoyed the wide variety of songs. But my non-Christian friend also attended. He didn't know any worship songs, so by the end of the conference, he never sang along with the songs once.

If you lead worship at conferences, pick fewer songs so that you can repeat them. That gives everyone a chance to sing, especially those who don't know any of the songs. Of course, if you know that everyone attending the conference is Christian and/or knows most of the songs, then adjust accordingly. But hopefully many of our conferences will have non-believers present to hear the good news!

Generally, the shorter the set, the fewer new songs you should use. For a set of six songs at my church, I would only teach one new song at most.

I also strategize as to where in a set to include an unfamiliar song. I do not end or start a set with an unfamiliar song. I want people to engage in worship with as few obstacles as possible. A new song presents an obstacle for some. I also want the final song of our worship sung with the greatest expressiveness. I don't want people inhibited in the final song by having to learn new words.

Where would I put an unfamiliar song? I put it usually after we have sung a beloved and well-known song. I do this because a new song requires the congregation to trust my song selection and to follow me into a new song. I would not ask the congregation to follow me into uncharted musical territory until after I have served them by leading a beloved worship song. Having been ministered to, the congregation trusts me as I lead them in newer songs.

Ultimately, I try to balance song selection from the perspective of the congregation. I aim to serve them through providing a rich selection of songs for their worship to God.

Balance Songs for Diverse Musical Tastes

You should also strive to balance musical tastes. The more diverse your congregation is, the more diverse their musical tastes. In my context, we have high diversity. Though most of our church comes from a Chinese heritage, we have rich diversity in age, culture, language, and values. Your leadership should pray about what musical style you want for your worship.

All worship music falls within a style or genre. You cannot avoid it. The moment you select a song, you have chosen a genre. The moment you arrange the song, you have chosen a style. So, pray and be intentional as you select and arrange your worship songs.

You might decide your worship service will have a focus on a particular worship music style. Perhaps you will have a majority of hymns accompanied by piano or organ. Perhaps you will have a style that reaches "young people." Or you might decide your worship service will have a broad musical range. Maybe you have families with older and younger folks. Then perhaps you want a more mainstream style with broader appeal.

Some people think that when you try to please everybody you end up pleasing nobody. There's some truth to this, but I have found the opposite to be true in leading worship. By leading a wider range of worship music, people respond to that service with openness toward other musical styles.

For example, my members who prefer hymns appreciate when I lead them. And since they see my attempts to include hymns in the service, they are more willing to try different styles. Such folks have come up to me after services to say, "Thanks for leading so many hymns. I know my kids like different music. I hope you can try to expose them to hymns even as I try to be more open to their music."

It is because of this that I strive for a balance between traditional hymns and contemporary worship songs. Again, by "balance" I do not necessarily mean an equal number. I think the reason my balance works with people is that I'm not simply putting in a token hymn or a token praise song. I want to expose the congregation to a fuller and richer repertoire of songs. I also stylistically blend hymns and choruses by updating musical arrangements of hymns, or by rearranging contemporary songs to work better with hymns.

It helps that I've been blessed with very gifted musicians on my worship teams over the years. I explain to them, "I want to arrange this hymn in a fresh way that appeals to newer Christians but also respects the traditional arrangements." This is a tough assignment, but one on which God has allowed our teams to work together.

Obviously, it's not always possible to balance all these issues in a single worship set. Some sets will not have any hymns. Some sets will not have any faster songs, and so forth. But what you cannot balance in a single set, you should balance over multiple sets. This leads us to our next section on balancing multiple sets.

WORKBOOK

Chapter Fifteen Questions

Your Heart: Do you enjoy introducing new songs to your congregation? How can you be strategic and intentional in your inclusion and introduction of new songs?

_____
_____
_____
_____
_____
_____
_____
_____
_____
_____

Your Church: How diverse is your congregation's musical tastes and preferences. (Consider age, socioeconomic class, race, etc.) How are you doing at representing these varied preferences in your worship service?

_____
_____
_____
_____
_____
_____
_____
_____
_____
_____

Your Commitment: Look over the sets you have used in the past month. Would you say that they are balanced with new vs. familiar and with the varied preferences of your congregation? In what ways can you improve the balance of your sets?

_____
_____
_____
_____

Chapter Fifteen Notes

PART THREE: SETS

Chapter Sixteen: Creating Balance for Multiple Sets

Not only should you strive for song balance within a single worship set, but I suggest you strive for balance over all your worship sets for a particular congregation. The types of balance you want for multiple sets include mood, theology, and "I" and "We" songs. After we discuss these types of balance, we will consider guidelines for balance.

Balance the Mood of Your Songs

You should balance out the mood of your songs. By mood, I mean the emotional state of the songs. As mentioned in earlier chapters, different praise songs express different emotions. Some praise songs are written to be happy, upbeat, and high energy. Other worship songs address remorse, repentance, or humility. You should balance your sets so that you do not focus only on one type of mood.

For example, some worship leaders seem to always lead happy songs of joy, thanksgiving, and praise. But they never lead songs that have to do with humility, mourning our sin, repentance, and pain. One indicator of such a leader is when people associate a worship leader with a specific type of worship set. Have you ever come to church and seen a particular lead worshiper onstage and thought, "Oh, this guy is leading today. I guess all the songs will be sentimental love songs." Or maybe you came to church and saw another worship leader in front and thought, "Oh, she's leading. I guess all the songs will be fast, clapping songs."

You get the idea.

Your worship leaders should lead worship with the full range of appropriate moods and emotions in Scripture—especially in the Psalms, which is a book of worship songs. You should lead moods appropriate to the season, the sermon, and the service. Assess your worship leaders. Do any of them show signs of favoring a specific mood? If so, point it out in a loving, gentle, but clear way. Ask them to balance this out over different worship sets. If people associate a particular mood with a particular worship leader, this may indicate that the leader has not provided a diverse enough range of moods when leading.

Balance the Theological Topics

You should balance out the theological topics of your songs. By theological topics, I mean what the worship songs are about. Your songs should reflect the fullness of our God and His attributes. Sing about salvation and redemption. Sing about forgiveness and grace. Sing about evangelism and fellowship. Sing about all the members of the Trinity. Sing about prayer and sing about worship. Sing about holiness and sing about joy. Sing about God's compassion for the poor. Sing about God's love for the weak. Sing about Jesus in our lives today and Jesus returning bodily in the future. Sing about as many topics as there are in the Bible! This may require us to find additional songs to reflect a fuller picture of God. We may have to draw from different worship resource sites. We may even have to write songs! Take a look at the songs your congregation sang the most in the past twelve months. How many topics do those songs address? Are there any topics missing? Do we sing not just about Jesus and the heavenly Father, but also about the Holy Spirit? What patterns or tendencies do you see when you review all the songs you've led in the past, say, six months?

Balance "I" Songs with "We" Songs

Observers of sociology have long pointed out the rugged individualism of Western culture, especially in the United States. While there is nothing wrong with a song written from an individual's perspective, we must remember that church is a body of believers.

Critics of contemporary worship songs point out that modern songs usually have the perspective where the worshipers are the subject. That is, the song's subject is the individual doing the singing—songs in which the singer says "I." Such songs say, "I love You" or "I need You" or "I worship You."

The point of this criticism is that modern worship is individualistic, especially in cultures like America. The modern worship environment is a darkened room where you can't see other people (except the worship team). And many modern worship leaders say things like, "Don't worry about the people around you. Just focus on God." I appreciate how this may relieve us from feeling embarrassed about our singing or self-conscious of how we sound, but we must be on our guard against making worship too individualistic.

Congregational worship is, by definition, a group of people worshiping together. For our songs to reflect that, we need songs in which a group is doing the singing—songs in which the singers say, "We."

Many contemporary worship songs are actually written for individual worship, not congregational worship. They were written by a single artist expressing worship as an individual to God. And because of the song's popularity or quality, worship leaders chose those songs for congregational worship. We need discernment here. As a corporate body, we should sing songs in which the congregation worships God together.

Requirements for Balance

Now that we have considered the types of balance we want for multiple worship sets, let's consider the requirements to achieve that balance.

Create Balance over Time

Creating balance over multiple sets requires that you lead multiple sets in the same congregation, and by that, I mean over a span of years. The balance I discuss above cannot be achieved in a single set, or even a few sets. That's not practical nor desirable.

Some of my worship sets have no hymns; others have mainly hymns. Some of my sets are very upbeat; other sets are almost all slow songs. Some of my sets are mainly about the cross, creation, or forgiveness. A single worship set cannot possibly include the range of balances we discussed above. That's why balancing out the mood, topics, and "I" vs "We" aspects of worship entails evaluating all the worship sets I have led in a particular congregation over a longer period of time than just a single week or even a single year.

I have led the same congregations in worship over years or even decades, so I can get away with any one set that appears less balanced, because the congregation knows me and my worship leadership. We're aiming for balance over a ministry of worship, not just for one Sunday.

Long-Serving Worship Leaders

This raises another requirement for balance over many sets: that worship leaders stay in a congregation for years. Most congregants favor long pastorates over short ones. Longer pastorates give both shepherd and flock time to learn to love one another. Assuming the pastor is qualified, everybody wins from a longer pastorate.

The same holds true for long-serving worship leaders. Stay in a congregation long enough to know the congregation. Work alongside your pastor long enough to develop a close-knit team relationship. Build the trust of your congregation and leadership. Learn what songs and music best serve your congregation. Serve them for a long time, as the Lord allows!

Keep a Record

This also means that you should keep a record of all your songs and worship sets. If you do not keep a record, how can you check your long-term balance?

Sometimes a person will come up to me after worship service and say, "We don't sing any hymns" or "We don't sing many fast songs" or "We haven't sung [a particular song] in a while." I usually just thank them for their feedback and say that I will look into it.

I keep a record of every song I've led so I can pull out

my record and check exactly what songs I have led. I may see that I have indeed fallen into a pattern. Or I may see that the observation did not fit with reality. Or I may learn that people have different expectations of what "enough" hymns, fast songs, slow songs, etc., means.

Sometimes people have selective memory. They only remember the times I did not include a particular type of song. One time a brother came up to me after Sunday service to complain "You don't lead hymns." In that situation, I tried to politely point out that I actually led two hymns that very morning—but they were late to service and missed them! In fact, I noticed that this dear brother was consistently late to church and would often miss out on many of the hymns I led!

If you want to check your song balance, you must keep a record of all your songs. I have a record of every worship song my congregation has sung for over ten years. When I sense we have an imbalance—be it theological, emotional, musical, etc.—I can work with my worship leaders by going over our records.

You've probably heard it said that people benefit from a balanced diet. Well, the same goes for worship songs. A congregation nourished in a balanced diet of different types, different topics, and different perspectives of worship songs can better enrich their understanding and praise of our amazing God.

Moreover, having a balance of worship songs does not just benefit the congregation. The worship leader who strives for balance will likely grow in his own leadership, his own skill, and his own worship of God. Having a record of worship songs also benefits leadership transitions. The leaders who followed after me were surprised to learn that we kept a record of all the songs we've sung for over a decade. They shared that it helped them transition into their worship leadership roles.

WORKBOOK

Chapter Sixteen Questions

Your Heart: What type of songs and sets speak to your personal walk with God and which ones do you tend to overlook? How have your own life experiences and personality created imbalance in your selection of worship music?

_____
_____
_____
_____
_____
_____
_____
_____
_____
_____

Your Church: Evaluate each person in your church who selects/leads music. Are they balanced in their choice and presentation of sets? If there are obvious gaps in the variety of mood or the gamut of their theological preferences, then consider how you can kindly encourage them to step out and try new songs for greater balance.

_____

_____

_____

_____

_____

_____

_____

_____

_____

_____

_____

Your Commitment: As described in this chapter, evaluate the worship sets you have used over the past 6-12 months. How is the balance in mood, theological truths, and individual vs. corporate focus? Particularly make note of any theological truths that may be missing from your repertoire and begin to look for songs that could fill in these gaps. Consider asking someone with theological background, like your pastor, to help you identify theological topics that may be lacking in your worship sets. If you have not already, devise a simple but effective system for keeping a record of all your worship sets. A searchable and sortable computer database/document will prove more helpful over the long term than hard copies.

_____

_____

_____

_____

_____

_____

_____

_____

_____

_____

Chapter Sixteen Notes

PART THREE: SETS

Chapter Seventeen:
End Worship with a Bang!

It's usually a good idea to select a closing song that the congregation knows well and enthusiastically sings. If there's any song of a set that the congregation should be fully engaged in, it should be the final song of the set.

Ending with a bang doesn't mean you always end with an upbeat, happy, driving song. It means ending with a song that the congregation can sing with total abandon, unencumbered by unfamiliar words or music.

Sometimes you want to end a worship service with a new song because the pastor requested it, or it just fits. What should you do? Remember, the principle I suggest here is to end the set with a familiar song. If you cannot replace that unfamiliar song, then you will need to familiarize the congregation with that song before the end of the worship service.

One way to do this is to lead that song earlier in the service. Perhaps you can sing the song for the congregation during the offering collection. Or, you can play the song while people file into the sanctuary. You can also teach the song earlier in the worship service.

I suggest teaching the song with a simple accompaniment to help people learn the melody. If the song has complex rhythms or lyrics, teach them at a slightly slower tempo so they can get the rhythm right. Even singing the song just one time helps most people learn the song.

Sometimes you may want to end the service with a new song, and you want them to have never sung that song before. What then? Don't do it.

"But I must," you say? No, you don't.

Why must you? Unless the song is simple enough or your congregation is musical enough, don't do it. Just don't do it. End the set with a song that most people can sing with freedom and focused attention on God.

Will It Fly?

After you've planned your worship set, step back and take a look at the whole order of service and worship songs. Ask yourself, "Is my congregation going to get into this set of songs? Are there songs or transitions in this set that will be rough? Is this worship set going to work?"

Again, we're not trying to manipulate emotions or undermine the work of the Holy Spirit. But like in preaching, a good pastor will look at his sermon manuscript before delivery and ask himself, "Will this sermon preach?" So, after your preparation, take a step back to answer this question, "Will it fly?"

If you're not sure how well a worship set will fly, then ask a trusted leader, pastor, or friend. If you do this regularly, you will likely identify those individuals who seem to have a knack for recognizing worship sets that serve your church well.

WORKBOOK

Chapter Seventeen Questions

Your Heart: Ending with a "bang" doesn't mean that the close of the service needs to be bigger and better than the rest of the service. How can a simple, well-known song meet the needs of the congregation better than a complex anthem?

_____
_____
_____
_____
_____
_____
_____
_____

Your Church: What does a typical "end" of your service look like? Is there an altar call? Does the final song lead to a closing prayer or does a prayer lead to a closing song? How can you fit these pieces together to end with strength and help each person focus as entirely on God as possible?

_____
_____
_____
_____
_____
_____
_____
_____
_____
_____

Your Commitment: Identify a few people in your church that you can call on when you need someone to look over your order of service and answer the "will it fly?" question with helpful feedback.

_____
_____
_____
_____

Chapter Seventeen Notes

Part Four:
Leading

PART FOUR: LEADING

Chapter Eighteen:
The True Worship Leader

The true worship leader of the service is not you. It's not your pastor. And it's not the one who opens the service in prayer. The Bible shows us that the true worship leader is the Holy Spirit.

When we pray as leaders before our worship services, I often pray for the heavenly Father to work through the true worship leader: the Holy Spirit. How does the Holy Spirit serve as our true, ultimate Worship Leader?

1. He convicts us of our sin and need for God (John 16:8).

2. He opens our spiritual eyes to see God's glory (1 Corinthians 2:10).

3. He illuminates us to the truths we should sing to God (John 16:13).

4. He helps us worship God in Spirit and in truth (John 4:24).

Lead with Your Demeanor As the Holy Spirit Guides You

We've defined worship leading as directing people toward the triune God. Since no one seeks God on their own, only the Holy Spirit truly directs people to God (Romans 3:11–12; Psalm 14:1–3). That said, we are also God's vessels, and how we respond to the Holy Spirit's leading in our lives will direct how our congregations follow our example.

To follow the leading of the Spirit in worship is more than just playing and singing particular songs. It also means seeking the Holy Spirit to guide your very mindset and mood. It means leading worship with your demeanor.

Your congregation will follow your demeanor. If I looked at your demeanor before you started the next song, could I guess what the song would be about? I should. Maybe not the exact song, but I should be able to guess the mood, content, and emotion of the next song by your demeanor.

If the next song conveys repentance over sins, then my body language should reflect that. If the next song is about joy coming to the world, I should look joyful. Beyond that, I should genuinely feel that joy!

Preparing for worship as leaders is more than just practicing and memorizing words. It's about the actions. You rehearse not just the music, but also the emotions. You lead the congregation not just in the melody and words, but also with moods and demeanor.

Would a congregation sing with joy if the worship team looked tired? Would a congregation sing with passion if the worship team looked bored? Would a congregation try to focus on God if the worship team seemed focused on trying to play the song correctly? Would a congregation feel excited to worship God at church if the worship team looked like they wished they were still in bed? The answer to all of these is, of course, no.

Remember, you sing not only to worship, but also to model. Lead not just with the music but lead with your demeanor.

Worship Goes Beyond the Sunday Service

Let's go back to the principle that worship involves our whole lives. Why would we want the Holy Spirit to lead our worship for one hour on Sundays if we don't want His leadership the rest of the week? We must yield to the Holy Spirit with all we are in order follow the Holy Spirit in corporate worship.

Whether or not you believe the Holy Spirit leads today through the gift of tongues or prophecy, all believers agree that the Spirit leads today in the hearts of true Christians and through God's Word. Let us follow the true Worship Leader in all aspects of our lives each day.

Spirit of God, lead us.

WORKBOOK

Chapter Eighteen Questions

Your Heart: Do you actively seek the leadership of the Holy Spirit to guide you throughout each phase of leading worship? Are you yielded to the Holy Spirit's leadership in *each* area of your life? How can you better model worship leading on the other days of the week besides Sunday?

_____

_____

_____

_____

_____

_____

_____

_____

_____

Your Church: Have your worship team take turns watching each other lead worship and give honest feedback on the demeanor of each leader. How can you help each other to be effective in worship when a team member is truly exhausted, not feeling well, or facing unusual stress or grief?

_____
_____
_____
_____
_____
_____
_____
_____
_____
_____

Your Commitment: Purpose to lead with your demeanor and to rely on the Holy Spirit, especially at those times when you don't naturally *feel* the appropriate emotions. How can obedience transcend feelings? What can you do in preparation for leading to help you truly feel the appropriate emotions?

_____
_____
_____

Chapter Eighteen Notes

PART FOUR: LEADING

Chapter Nineteen:
Orderliness and Expressiveness in Worship

I've heard many worship leaders tell their congregations, "Don't worry about how you look or sound to others as we sing this next song. It's just between you and God."

I understand why this encouragement may help. We are concerned about what others think of our worship. We are concerned about how well we sing, how we look while singing, and the opinions of others. However, the exhortation not to care about what others think has sometimes led to excessive displays of emotion during congregational singing that distracts of detracts others from worshiping God.

One time, in a worship service I attended, two or three people in a room of about 300 decided they wanted to continue singing the same worship song a few more times. This happened while the worship leader was trying to lead the congregation in prayer. You can imagine how this produced a distracting, if not awkward, situation.

After the service had concluded, some of the church leaders approached those few individuals. The leaders asked those who had continued singing not to do so while the worship leader was trying to pray or close the service. Their behavior was making the worship more chaotic rather than orderly. This group of people responded, "But we were just worshiping the way we felt we should. It shouldn't matter what others think if we are worshiping God."

Should we care about what others think about our worship? Should it matter how we appear as long as we worship God in our hearts, whatever that means?

I believe that God cares not only about what we sing, but also about how we sing. Appropriate worship praises God according to His glory. God is great, so our songs should sing of His greatness. God is love, so our songs should sing of His love. But God's character should inform not only the message of our songs, but also the manner in which we praise Him.

God's Character and the Manner of Worship

God's character teaches us many lessons about the manner of our worship. But for today's generation, I would focus on one aspect: orderly worship.

The Bible teaches that our worship should be orderly, especially congregational worship. "For God is not a God of confusion but of peace" (1 Corinthians 14:33). The context of this text involves people worshiping through prophecy or speaking in tongues. Paul's point is that worship must be orderly, even if we have a word from the Lord. Actually, Paul's point is that worship must be orderly, *especially* when we have a word from the Lord.

If apostles with a word from the Holy Spirit should maintain order, then so should the church today. This is so "all things [are] done for building up... so that all may learn and be encouraged..." (1 Corinthians 14:26b, 31b).

Order Is Not Oppressive

Orderly worship does not entail the absence of passion or emotion. Orderly worship does not entail quenching the Holy Spirit. Paul's instruction to maintain order does not conflict with David's instruction to shout for joy or worship with gladness (Psalm 100).

Biblical worship should not be chaotic nor disorderly. But neither should it be stoic and repressed. That's because God in His character is not those things. God is passionate, but God is controlled.

We need not choose between expressive worship and orderly worship. Rather, biblical worship expresses itself in an orderly manner. And biblical worship orders itself to fully express praise to God. Therefore, worship leaders should lead people to express passionate worship that honors our God of order and peace.

WORKBOOK

Chapter Nineteen Questions

Your Heart: Reflect on a time when you were trying to worship in an environment where the desire for "order" led to legalism and repression. Then consider a time when a lack of order in worship led to chaos and a glorification of the flesh. How can a worship leader find and maintain a biblical balance?

_____

_____

_____

_____

_____

_____

_____

_____

_____

_____

Your Church: Does your church tend more toward order or spontaneity? How can you encourage the other without becoming out of balance?

_____
_____
_____
_____
_____
_____
_____
_____
_____
_____

Your Commitment: How can order in your worship preparation lead to order in your worship presentation? How does the order of the worship leader influence the congregation? Choose an area to work on orderliness this week; it could be the sorting and storing of music, the rehearsal preparation, or the physical order of the front platform, etc.

_____
_____
_____

Chapter Nineteen Notes

PART FOUR: LEADING

Chapter Twenty:
Good Repute Takes Time

A worship leader can earn a poor reputation with one bad worship set. But one earns a reputation as a good worship leader over a long period of time.

As I shared previously, when a parishioner came to me after service one week claiming I "never" lead any hymns, I took his point to heart, despite the fact that he was incorrect. Even though I had a record of every song I had led, and could have pointed out his error or attempted to defend myself, that's not a good way to receive feedback. I needed to learn from this encounter.

For whatever reason, this brother had perceived I did not lead any hymns even though I had included at least one hymn in every worship set I led. I decided I needed to pay more attention to this dynamic. Here's what I discovered as I tried to incorporate his feedback.

First, people would often miss the hymn because we sang the hymn first for Sunday service. In my church, many arrived after the first song, so those folks never sang the hymns.

Second, I often led only part of a hymn. In order to save

time or to match a theme, I would use only the chorus, or I would leave out a verse or two.

Third, I didn't play the hymn with a traditional arrangement or instrument. We usually used a contemporary arrangement. These partial hymns or rearranged hymns did not register as a hymn to some people.

In some cases, these instances were worse than not doing the hymn at all. Some people felt that we had taken their beloved hymn and "ruined it" by using a modern instrument or arrangement.

So, I began to place hymns in sets when most people would be present. I began to start the hymns with a more recognizable "hymn-ish" arrangement on the piano instead of the guitar. And whenever I could, I would ask this brother if he thought I was doing more hymns.

Now, this was not my main concern when I selected songs. I did not approach worship planning with the question, "How can I appease my hymn-loving brother?" No. I still tried to select and arrange songs in a way that I thought best served our congregation as a whole, that fit well with the topic of the Sunday sermon, and that my team could play well. But I did also look over my sets with this lens to see if I included recognizable hymns.

Then something funny happened. One Sunday, I had done what I usually did: picked what I hoped to be the best songs for that set. And it didn't occur to me until after I led that set that every single song was a hymn. (In those days, a "hymn" was loosely defined as a song whose author had already died or was a song that people over sixty years old had sung as children.) This brother approached me after the worship set, smiled, and profusely thanked me for serving him in his worship of God. He became a supporter.

After that, I noticed a change in him. He engaged more in worship—even when I didn't lead hymns. I saw him try harder to sing along to modern worship songs. He began to point out to his like-minded friends that I did, in fact, attempt to balance both older and newer songs for our services.

This good reputation took many Sundays to cultivate. And by God's grace, I enjoyed a wonderful relationship with the older congregation members in that church for years to come. I enjoyed that good reputation for so long, I forgot how long it took to earn a good reputation until God moved me to a new church.

I committed plenty of leadership missteps (both in worship leading as well as pastoral leading) in my early days of the new pastorship. I'd forgotten how much time and energy I had spent building up trust with my previous congregation. To some people, I came off prideful. I'm sure that I was, but that was not the whole story. I needed to remember that a good reputation takes many Sundays to build. And because I was new to the church, I would have to build that up again week by week.

Age and musical preference are just examples of situations you'll face in growing your worship ministry. The purpose of this chapter is to teach you that leading worship is a pastoral service. It requires time and energy to build up trust and credibility. Take heart in any feedback you receive from your parishioners. You're learning to worship together.

And remember that leading worship requires the patience to listen to the needs and preferences of your people. Like your creditability, that patience comes with time and practice.

WORKBOOK

Chapter Twenty Questions

Your Heart: How do you respond to criticism or complaints about your worship selection or style? What is your inward attitude and your outward response? How do you show pastoral care for those who may be critical or selfish about their musical preferences for worship?

_____

_____

_____

_____

_____

_____

_____

_____

Your Church: What are the main dividing issues in your church—age, musical preference, etc.? Have these historically been major or minor differences in your congregation?

_____
_____
_____
_____
_____
_____
_____
_____
_____
_____

Your Commitment: Talk to a seasoned pastor or worship leader about their experiences building up a good reputation. How did it take time and how did they win their critics over with patience and practice?

_____
_____
_____
_____

Chapter Twenty Notes

PART FOUR: LEADING

Chapter Twenty-One:
No Mini-Sermons Needed

Though believers hunger for God's Word (Psalm 119:20), that's no reason for the worship leader to preach a homily during a worship set. Unless otherwise directed, I urge our worship leaders to speak as little as possible.

Of course, some words are necessary. Worship leaders must offer words of direction as to what and when to sing next. It's appropriate that worship leaders give practical instructions such as "Turn to page 416 in your hymnal" or "We're going to teach you a new song." And worship leaders should feel free to lead the congregation in appropriate prayer.

But aside from those necessities, speak as little as possible. If you speak more, then let it be the necessary words of directing where and when to sing the next song. The words of the songs, if well-written, should suffice.

If you wish to speak more, use Scripture. Why say something banal and overused like "Let's sing this next song with all our hearts," when you could read aloud from Psalm 103:1, "Bless the LORD, O my soul, and all that is within me, bless his holy name"?

I won't call it sinful to give introductory remarks before each song, especially before songs with archaic words or expressions of some hymns. Hopefully, a worship leader speaks to edify, and not to fill silence, or to merely stall while the musicians change their music. Weigh each word before the Lord. "Be not rash with your mouth, nor let your heart be hasty to utter a word before God, for God is in heaven and you are on earth. Therefore let your words be few" (Ecclesiastes 5:2).

Worship Leading as Priestly Role, Not Prophetic Role

In the book of Joshua, the Levites were given the privilege of carrying the Ark of the Covenant across the Jordan River, leading the people of Israel into the Promised Land (Joshua 3). The worship leaders were consecrated by God and called to go first.

But the Levites rarely (or never) instigated change. They had to remain faithful, so that when God brought about change through prophets or other leaders, the Levites were ready to perform as instructed.

Today, all true Christians are a royal priesthood and thus, point people towards a relationship with God. But congregational worship leaders seem to have a more explicit priestly role.

This is different than having a prophetic role, in which individuals challenged people to radically reorient their lives in accordance with God's commands.

The congregational worship leader's role in a church, who humbly serves in leading worship of God, seems to me closer to that of a priest. The pastor-teacher today seems to be closer to having a prophetic role of calling people towards repentance back to God.

What does this all mean? Well, if you are a worship leader, yet you feel a compulsion to challenge people to come back to God, you should by all means explore that calling to see if it is from the Lord. But that calling may fit more with an evangelist or preacher than a worship leader.

Someone might say, "But I write songs which are prophetic and call people to a radical devotion to God." I recognize that songs can have timely and prophetic messages to them. But as I wrote above, in those cases let the words and music of the song do the speaking. I have found that the songs with the greatest impact did not need me to provide commentary to have their impact.

To use the modern worship leader role in a prophetic or teaching role may be a mismatch. If you feel called to preach, then consider becoming a preacher in the worship service.

> *But you are a chosen race, a royal priesthood, a holy nation, a people for his own possession, that you may proclaim the excellencies of him who called you out of darkness into his marvelous light.*
> —*1 Peter 2:9*

My Story

I led worship almost every Sunday for several years at my current church. That gave me an opportunity to serve and influence the congregation in significant ways. But until I became a pastor and preacher, much of my role would be responding to the congregation rather than directing it.

I love leading worship, and I miss it. As a worship leader, my job has a priestly role to meet my congregation where they are and help direct them to God. But as a teacher and pastor, my job has a prophetic role to meet my congregation where they are and help move them forward to God through the power of His Word.

Each role has different callings. Both are important and ordained by God.

If you're trying to effect transformation in the lives of your people, then leading worship singing is not the best way to do that (especially in Asian American contexts). God ordained that the proclamation of His Word through the work of the Holy Spirit would transform people (Romans 10:13–17).

In the Bible, people didn't sing before major transformative experiences. They sang *after* those experiences—such as singing after Red Sea parted and swallowed the Egyptians (Exodus 15) or when Mary celebrated with Elizabeth after being told she would give birth to the Christ (Luke 1:46–56).

So if you feel called to a prophetic role, you may want to explore serving as a teacher or evangelist. If you want to continue in a worship leading role, then recognize that your role is one that requires you to mostly respond and not so much effect change. If you're like me, you may sense God calling you to both of these roles. Understanding this may help you discern the calling God has for your life.

WORKBOOK

Chapter Twenty-One Questions

Your Heart: How often do you speak during the worship service other than giving needed instructions? When you speak, what is the purpose of your communication? If you have a heart for teaching or preaching, in what context could you better exercise those gifts?

_____

_____

_____

_____

_____

_____

_____

_____

_____

_____

Your Church: How can the responsive ministry of worship enhance the transformative ministry of preaching? How have you seen cooperation between these two ministries at your church?

_____
_____
_____
_____
_____
_____
_____
_____
_____

Your Commitment: Make a list of Scriptures that fit with the various moods and themes of your worship sets as well as the various parts of the order of service. This will be used in the next chapter as well.

_____
_____
_____
_____
_____

_____
_____
_____
_____
_____
_____

Chapter Twenty-One Notes

PART FOUR: LEADING

Chapter Twenty-Two: Worship with Scripture

Until I come, devote yourself to the public reading of Scripture...
—*1 Timothy 4:13a*

Incorporating Scripture is an important component to planning a worship service. The Bible instructs us to read Scripture in public worship. Jesus himself modeled how Scripture should be read in the corporate worship of God. (See Luke 4:16-17). Thus, we should incorporate Scripture reading into our contemporary church services.

Modern worship services have many options to incorporate Scripture. You can put Scripture up on a screen for the congregation to read. You can have someone read Scripture. You can also have a responsive Scripture reading. By whatever means you incorporate Scripture, it makes sense to do so intentionally in a meaningful and respectful way.

If you want to project Scripture on a screen for the congregation to read, you can do this in different ways. You can project Scripture onto a screen during a song or in between songs. This can be done with musical accompaniment or in silence for people to read themselves.

One verse I would project in silence while serving as a worship leader was Habakkuk 2:20. Imagine a service where, after the final song and before the benediction, the congregation sees this verse on the screen as the band ceases playing:

> But the LORD is in His holy temple;
> Let all the earth keep silence before Him.

A second way to incorporate Scripture into worship is with a reading. A worship team member can read a brief Scripture. I often prefer someone other than the main leader to read. People appreciate a literal change in voice.

A third way to incorporate Scripture into worship is through responsive reading. That's when the leader reads a portion of Scripture and then the congregation (leader included) responds with a portion of Scripture. This method works well for longer selections of Scripture. This method also engages the congregation more.

I have not read a book on how to do this, but here is what I do. I select a Psalm or other text that has natural breaks or lines. I then divide up the text into portions to be read by the leader and the congregation. I try to be sensitive to the context, to the paragraph breaks, and to the genre. For examples of this, see the Samples of Call to Worship in Appendix C of this book.

It helps to think of a responsive reading as another movement in the worship set. It's a non-singing song.

I tend to place responsive readings in between song movements. I select a Scripture that matches the theme or topic. I also select a text that fits the mood or dynamic level of the music. For example, if my set is building up, then I choose a more poignant Scripture, such as Psalm 147:6: "Great is the Lord and mighty in power, his understanding has no limit," (NIV). If my set is settling down, I choose accordingly. For example, I might use this Scripture to settle people down into humble reflection: "Humble yourselves, therefore, under God's mighty hand... Cast your anxiety on him because he cares for you," (1 Peter 5:6-7, NIV). Notice how both of these verses include the idea of God's might, yet one is meant to uplift, and the other is meant to humble us.

Of all the songs you could sing, this "song" of Scripture reading sings best because it's the very words of God breathed out as Scripture. Arrange it as you would any other song, with the same expectation, reverence, and care you would give to the prettiest tune.

Where do you find the Scriptures to incorporate? Ideally, in your own personal reading and study of Scripture. Often, the best sermons flow out of the life of preachers as they read the Bible for their own personal growth. Similarly, a worship leader should be regularly studying, memorizing, and reflecting upon Scripture in his own personal devotional life. And as he does so, he may find many passages to choose from for corporate Scripture reading.

WORKBOOK

Chapter Twenty-Two Questions

Your Heart: The best way to incorporate Scripture into corporate worship is to incorporate it first into your personal worship. How much time are you spending reading the Word, memorizing and meditating on the Word, and praying and praising through the Word? Evaluate your personal dedication to Scripture. How will you continue to grow in this area?

_____

_____

_____

_____

_____

_____

_____

_____

_____

Your Church: Work with the members of your worship team on expressive reading of Scripture and plan for each of them to take a turn in worshiping with Scripture.

_____
_____
_____
_____
_____
_____
_____
_____
_____
_____

Your Commitment: Look at Appendix C and study the various Calls to Worship. Pick out a responsive reading (or craft your own) to use with your congregation in the coming month. If this has not been a regular part of your worship, you may need to instruct your congregation, and be sure to model enthusiastic reading as the leader.

_____
_____
_____
_____
_____

Chapter Twenty-Two Notes

PART FOUR: LEADING

Chapter Twenty-Three:
Solo Performances and Interludes

Old-timers in my church used to frown whenever the band played a musical interlude or a solo performance during worship. "Shouldn't we direct our attention to God?" they would ask. "Doesn't a solo point us toward the skills of the musician or singer?"

They raise a good point. "Besides," they'd say, "what's the congregation supposed to do during a solo?" They felt like solos and long musical interludes were showy. They feared we were saying, "Look at me, I'm playing a solo!"

Nowadays, musical solos can be found as an integral part of many worship services. Recent attendees to American churches regularly see worship teams play solos, jams, and riffs. It doesn't occur to them to even ask, "What does a solo have to do with corporate worship?"

Nevertheless, we still ask the question, "What's the point of a solo during worship?"

For that matter, what's the point of a choir singing an anthem or a call to worship? What should people actually *do* or *look at* or *think about* during those times? Precious few worship leaders and pastors educate their congregations. Maybe because they've never asked the question either. Or if they have asked the question, maybe they don't have a good answer. Or if they have a good answer, it doesn't occur to them to tell the congregation.

By a "solo", I do not mean when a particular song leader is the only one singing into the microphone to lead the congregation. (I will further discuss this in Chapter Twenty-Six on "Worship Cues for the Band".) I also do not mean that it's only one person leading the congregation. What I really mean by "solo" is a performance by one (or more) of the worship team when the congregation is expected to watch and listen to the singer sing the song. Often this happens when a vocalist sings lyrics which are not projected on a screen or otherwise made available to the congregation.

So, I will address two questions. First, should we allow for solos/performances during worship services? Second, what should people do during choir pieces, musical offertories, musical solos, and the like?

Should We Have Solo Performances?

There are good and bad reasons for having solos during worship services. Whether you should include a solo (be it choral, instrumental, etc.) depends on at least these two factors: your motivation (or intention) and your situation.

1. What is your motivation or intention? Is your motivation to let people know how good you are at playing or singing? That's not a good reason. Is your intention to enrapture people with the beauty of God captured in the music? If so, that sounds acceptable.

The proper intention for offering a solo or instrumental to God should be the same for any offering to God. We offer our treasures to God as an act of worship, devotion, and gratefulness. If we can offer animals, grains, and money to God, then surely we can offer our art and music. Music has the power to evoke emotions, images, and ideas. Beautiful music can help people focus on the beauty of God. Don't misunderstand me. I am not saying that music makes people worship God. Only the Holy Spirit can move sinful people to worship a holy God. But the right music can point people in the right direction.

Some folks love the grand old buildings of ancient churches. The immensity, the expanse, the solidness of the stones, all serve to bring people to a place of reverence for the transcendent God. The same can be true for a beautiful solo. I may not even know the song, but the music is so beautiful it hurts. I think it hurts because you don't want it to end, but you know it has to. Or maybe it hurts because it captures how you want to worship God but can't. At least, not yet in this life.

I remember sitting in a summer camp in Texas. We were singing a well-known song, using a well-known arrangement. But this time, there was a new girl on the worship team. And as we sang the song, I heard what to me was the most beautiful voice I've ever heard. The beauty was more than just the tone, but in the act of singing a beautiful song of worship to God. At that moment, the beauty of that voice singing to God made me want to worship God all the more. I still get moved and feel chills when I recall that experience.

But that's the power of art, and in particular, music. The beauty of music or the truth of a sermon or the power of forgiveness point to the God who is Beauty, Truth, and Power.

2. Will a solo or interlude help or hinder people's attention on God? If musical solos help people worship by directing their attention to God, then that's fine. If solos distract people, then you should not use them. Consider your situation and make the best decision based on that.

In one of my previous churches, the congregation had no issue when a choir member sang a solo in the service. But many disapproved of a solo in the worship set. I pointed out this apparent inconsistency and asked for a reason we allowed one type of solo but not the other. No one could provide a good reason.

Since no one could provide a good reason to exclude solos, did I start including solos? No. There are other considerations in my situation. Just because no one could provide a logical reason did not mean to go ahead and include solos. Much of the congregation disapproved of solos during worship, regardless of whether or not they could articulate a reason. I noticed that whenever I included a brief solo or slightly longer musical introduction, people shifted uncomfortably in the pews. I could sense people wondering whether God was going to strike the soloist down for such self-aggrandizing behavior.

So, I decided against solos. Even song intros were only a few bars long—the minimum length needed to establish key and tempo. Songs ended moments after the last words were sung. This may reveal more about the musical expectations of my congregation at the time. They were concerned that anytime the congregation was not singing along to the music, that the attention was turning too much to the "performers" on the stage.

But situations can change. Over time, I found I could stretch out song introductions a little here or there. Over time, I began to lengthen the ends of songs, drawing out the music. I choose to do this with hymns or other songs the congregation liked.

Later on, I noticed that people didn't frown when I had a slightly longer "outro" or inserted a few bars of instrumental after the bridge. Eventually, the congregation came to welcome longer song introductions, interludes, and postludes.

I believe the congregation came to embrace extended

musical interludes and solos because I gave them time to deal with the change. I also served them by letting them worship with solos for songs they loved to sing.

Like I said above, in the current state of corporate musical worship, it seems like the norm is to have song intros and outros and interludes in which the congregation does not sing for many, many bars of music. So this current generation may not question why we have those times of music compared to the "old days" when the only introduction was when the organist played the last few bars of the hymn before everyone started singing.

How Do We Worship During a Solo Performance?

Have you ever heard a worship leader tell the congregation to "meditate on this song" as the band plays? I have heard (and said) this cliché too many times to count. Ironic since I'm not sure what it really means.

It can mean so many things. Does it mean I sing silently while the band plays? Does it mean I picture Jesus hanging on a cross? What should I meditate on if the lyrics of a song say, "You are beautiful beyond description?"[11] That line basically says I can't comprehend God's beauty—so then, what am I supposed to think about?

As the worship leader, you should work with your pastor to teach people how to worship through meditation and music. This does not need to be unbiblically mystical. The Bible teaches that the "meditations of my heart" should be pleasing to God (Psalm 19:14). Ask your pastor to consider preaching on worship, meditation of Scripture, and how to meditate during solos.

Expounding on the topics of biblical reflection and meditation lie beyond the scope of this project, but here are a few suggestions you as the worship leader can offer to your congregation. Try them. See how things go.

Evaluate them with your worship teams and your church leaders.

Suggestions for worship during solos/instrumentals:

- Read through the words.
- Listen to others sing the words for you.
- Pray about the message of the song.
- Pray for people to worship God.
- Help the people confess their sins to God.
- Ask God to change you.

Are You Kidding Me?

I've spent over a thousand words on whether or not we should have solos in church worship services. Perhaps many readers are wondering, "Are you kidding me? Is this even an issue? Is this worth arguing over? Didn't we hash this out in the Eighties during the so-called 'worship wars'?" If that's you, then I suspect solos pose no problem for you or your church.

But the fact is that many churches struggle with this issue. And these churches might want to consider a transition to more contemporary musical forms and styles. This is not easy, especially for churches with a long, cherished history. If you are in this group, then I pray the Lord will give you patience, courage, and grace as you work through this issue with your congregation.

WORKBOOK

Chapter Twenty-Three Questions

Your Heart: How do "performances" of solos or interludes aid you in your personal worship? (Or if they don't, how and why do they hinder you?) How can you teach others to worship through these musical forms also?

_____
_____
_____
_____
_____
_____
_____
_____
_____
_____

Your Church: Is the environment in your church welcoming to solos or put off by them? How can you patiently help a cautious church embrace this form of worship and grow through it? If your church already welcomes and enjoys solos, how can you ensure that the focus remains on the Lord vs. a performance/performer?

_____

_____

_____

_____

_____

_____

_____

_____

_____

_____

Your Commitment: Do a word study on the phrase "meditations of my heart." (Psalm 19:14; Psalm 49:3). What does this teach about meditative worship?

_____

_____

_____

_____

_____

Chapter Twenty-Three Notes

PART FOUR: LEADING

Chapter Twenty-Four: Memorize Your Sets

I once played with a band that had all the usual gear with one exception: They didn't have music stands.

"Don't you need the music?" I asked the main leader.

"No, I just need the key the song is in."

Whoa...

As an amateur musician, this concept surprised and startled me. It surprised me because, up to that point, I couldn't imagine having no music in front of me.

But as I practiced songs and grew musically, I realized I looked less at the music on my stand. Instead, I would look more at my bandmates to keep us together. I was more aware of the congregation I was leading. And I was able to freely express my worship through music and leading. All this because I had come to the point where I did not need—no, did not want—sheet music.

I realized none of the musicians I admired in performances (or "musical offerings" as we call it in churches) and in well-led worship services used sheet music.

As a preacher, the same holds true. The best sermons and speeches I've listened to were those where the preacher did not use notes. If the preacher did use notes, the most engaging parts of the sermon were when the preacher looked up from the notes and spoke God's Word directly at us.

No Sheet Music, Are You Serious?

Telling a worship leader not to use sheet music is like telling a preacher he can't use notes. Most preachers I know agree that, in general, if you can preach a sermon without looking at notes, you will better engage the listeners. Yet this requires more work and preparation. It's scary, but if you can pull it off, you reap significant benefits.

You have memorized countless songs and information in your life. You've memorized the alphabet song, your address, and your "math facts" (aka multiplication tables). You may also have memorized more complex information. You may follow a sport and know your favorite athlete's stats by heart. You may love watching movies and have entire scenes memorized line by line. The same is true of music.

You can memorize your songs if you practice.

Don't expect to do this in a few weeks. Strive for it as you go about your usual worship ministry. I believe that you will find that if you intentionally work at this, you will succeed. In fact, I suggest that a worship team practice together to the point that they don't need sheet music.

Steps to Leading Without Sheet Music

How does a worship team take steps to leading without music?

1. Practice, practice, practice. Many worship leaders respond with uncertainty to the idea of leading without sheet music. They fear they will make a mistake, forget where they are in the song, and then go totally blank. That's understandable.

But the challenge to lead without music resembles preaching without notes or driving without a GPS. One need only more practice of the right kind.

You can lead without sheet music. You really can. I bet there are whole verses or even songs during which you never once look at the music. You may feel more secure if you can turn to the music, but you probably don't need it as much as you think you do.

To lead without sheet music, you must practice without sheet music. Try this. During an upcoming worship practice, surprise the team by saying you will now rehearse a well-known song with no music. Pick the song the team knows best. Just try playing without sheet music and see what happens.

If you can play the whole song just fine, that's fantastic. If you can't, go back and look at what parts you had trouble remembering. Then try the whole exercise again in the next rehearsal. I believe you will see improvement.

2. Lower your music stands. Lower them so much that it's hard to sing and play properly while looking at the music. Tell your band to play as much as they can and look down at the music only when necessary. Just be sure you place the stands low enough so that it's inconvenient to see the music. People will feel disinclined to look down and eventually get used to not looking at the music.

You can lower your music stands even more by placing the sheet music on the floor. It's very difficult and inconvenient to play or sing music while trying to read music laying on the floor by your feet.

Again, if you need to look, the music is there. Otherwise, make it hard to use the music so that the team learns to play without it.

3. Set a goal. You will never get anywhere if you don't set a goal. You can tell your team that on a certain date, you will play that entire set without sheet music. Maybe you will set a goal to lead a single song without music. Maybe you will lead the entire worship set. Set a goal and after you reach that goal, set another one.

As your team works hard at learning to lead without music, you will discover many of the benefits mentioned above for why to lead without sheet music.

How to Lead with Sheet Music

If your team is still new to playing music together (or their instruments in general), it may be too soon to eliminate the sheet music. If you must use sheet music, here are some tips to reduce distraction and the page-turning-pause.

1. Eliminate the pause. Sheet music requires time to adjust. After you finish one song, you have to change the page by turning, sliding, dropping, or swiping. That takes time and draws attention. Always have both the current song and the next song on the stand so the player can see what song comes next.

You can have a vocalist, or anyone else close enough with free hands, adjust the music. If you use electronic tablets to show your music, you can purchase Bluetooth foot pedals to turn pages, thus removing time needed to stop playing and change sheet music. My practice was to always have a vocalist beside me to adjust my music every time I started a new song. (You can also shrink the music so that multiple songs fit on one sheet.)

2. Have another instrument introduce the song while you adjust your music. (This also works if you need to adjust a guitar capo. Instead of the congregation watching you adjust a capo in silence, have the piano start the next song.)

What About All Those Verses?

What if you need music because a song has so many verses? Then use a card or sheet of paper with only the lyrics for that particular song. Ideally, all I have with me on the platform is a list of the songs for the set, and the key each song is in. I have usually memorized the lyrics, chords, and arrangement.

Five Benefits to Leading Without Sheet Music

Leading without sheet music offers several benefits:

1. You will grow musically. First and foremost, if you aim for the target of going without sheet music, you will benefit by pushing yourself musically. You will find that there are some common chord patterns. As you play without music, you may gain more confidence as you find you rely less on the sheet music and more on feeling the chord or lyrical progressions. This may take months, but it's worth it.

2. You can focus on leading worship rather than playing music. You have to work hard before something becomes easy and natural. An experienced ice skater doesn't think about what foot to put out next. An experienced driver doesn't pause to consider how to activate a turn signal. An experienced basketball player is one who can dribble the ball without thinking about it. Why? Because these skills that once seemed so difficult have become second nature. They must become second nature because they have more important things to think about.

Consider this. Imagine you did not need to look at the lyrics, the music, or the music stands during worship leading. What do you look at instead? You can watch your teammates to keep them musically together. You can watch the congregation to see how they are singing along. You can check if the projected lyrics are correct. You can focus on worshiping God in your own heart.

Any of these tasks are hard when you don't have to look at the music. And they become impossible to do if you are glued to your sheet music.

3. You can transition songs better. If you don't need the music, you can transition more quickly to the next song. Can you imagine this scene? The congregation just sang passionately. The band has ended the song. What happens next? What is everybody doing? In my experience, everyone looks at the team leader as he switches his sheet music for the next song.

This gets me every time. If a leader wants to have silence in between songs, that's fine. If a leader wants people to pause before the next hymn, that's fine. But let's not pause after every song just because the team needs to change the sheet music!

This applies especially when the songs are upbeat. Imagine we just finished an upbeat song and we are going to sing another upbeat song next. Two upbeat songs in a row—what a time for energy, excitement, anticipation! But if in between those upbeat songs we wait through five seconds of silence when all eyes are watching the guitar player change his music, that momentum is lost. Let's practice so we can transition songs better, especially fast songs.

4. Eliminate visual clutter and distractions. In most churches, the platform (really the "stage" but many churches want to avoid that word) has numerous items:

speakers, feedback monitors, cables, flowers, instruments, altar, pulpit, and people. The music stands and paper only add to a sense of clutter that can distract the worshiper.

Furthermore, worship leaders without a music stand between them and the congregation are more accessible, natural, and connected to the rest of the church.

I said earlier that churches prefer the term "platform" to "stage." Perhaps people want to avoid the notion that the worship service is a performance. I see the platform as a stage for the saints as they worship the audience of One. Let's remove as much clutter from the stage as possible. That includes removing unused mic stands and instrument cases from the stage as well.

5. You have freedom to change songs as needed. If your team can play a repertoire from memory, in multiple keys, then you have the most freedom to change songs on the spot. Sometimes the preacher will say to the worship leader right before the service begins, "I should have asked you before, but can you lead a different song after my sermon?"

Or maybe you decide on a different response song as you listen to the sermon. If your team has memorized a repertoire of songs, you have the option of singing that unplanned song.

Note: If you do decide to change a song at the last moment, remember that the lyrics operator must also have the ability to project unplanned songs quickly. Software and familiarity with worship songs should help the person controlling the slides.

If you are a seasoned musician, then the thought of playing and leading without music may not seem difficult to you. I suppose I wrote this chapter for those musicians who are less experienced and/or less confident. Unless we are in a larger church with many musical resources, most of our worship teams may people who feel like they have a lot to learn musically. As a fellow amateur musician, I encourage you to take steps to continue to develop your craft and ability in music. Developing yourself into a musician who does not need to have music to lead worship is a worthy milestone to reach.

WORKBOOK

Chapter Twenty-Four Questions

Your Heart: Look at the list of benefits to playing without sheet music. Which one would have the greatest impact on you as a worship leader? How will the freedom of memorization outweigh the convenience or comfort of sheet music?

_____
_____
_____
_____
_____
_____
_____
_____
_____

Your Church: Look at the platform or "stage" of your church during the middle of a worship service. Try to see it as if you were a guest. Where is there visual clutter? How can the "stuff" be minimized and all unnecessary items kept hidden?

_____
_____
_____
_____
_____
_____
_____
_____
_____
_____

Your Commitment: Plan to take a step this week toward paperless worship leading. What song(s) have you already memorized or almost memorized? Is there a song that your entire team can do from memory? Start with one song, then move to a set. When one set is mastered, utilize that one and begin working on another. Create incentives for your team to encourage them as they take this extra effort.

_____
_____

Chapter Twenty-Four Notes

PART FOUR: LEADING

Chapter Twenty-Five:
Introducing an Unfamiliar Song

Leading an unfamiliar song to a congregation differs from leading a song the congregation knows. If you want the congregation to sing a new song, you must teach them the song.

Right off the bat, the thought of needing to *teach* a song may seem odd. In some congregations and cultures, music is such a common part of life that it seems like most people can sing in tune, harmonize, and keep a beat. But in my context, the typical person never sang songs at home or on car rides. In my household growing up, my parents did not know how to read music or play an instrument. And as a kid, I never saw my parents go to concerts, buy music albums, or listen to music at home.

I realize this may be uncommon, and may even become rarer in our world of digital music. Nevertheless, there will always be folks in our congregations who would not consider themselves "musical people." They are more self-conscious about singing, unsure about their voice, and never learned to play a musical instrument or read music.

Since worship leaders are called to serve their entire congregation, we should learn to introduce and teach a new song to our congregations, especially to those people who don't think of themselves as "musical people."

Worship leaders should arrange unfamiliar songs in appropriate ways to teach people how to sing them. Playing the song at full speed and with full instrumentation is not teaching. Teaching usually means using less instrumentation, so people can better learn the melody. It means going at a slower tempo, so they better learn the rhythm. It may also mean singing the bridge more than once so they can actually learn it.

Tell the congregation you want to teach them a new song. This informs people that if the song is unfamiliar to them, they're not alone. Then I do just that: Proceed to *teach* them the song. I play it for them and let them listen first. I sing a line and have them repeat it. I tell them what the words mean. If needed, I slow the tempo and repeat the trickier parts. I teach the congregation the song.

Tips for Teaching Songs

Here are three tips for teaching the congregation new songs:

1. Don't end or start with new songs. I've already shared the point about what songs to start with (songs that focus people into a heart of worship).

2. Lead the song twice in the same service. In my church, we have two worship sets. The opening set we sing in the beginning of the service. The closing set we sing after the sermon and right before the benediction. I encourage our worship leaders that if they're teaching a new song, to teach it in the opening set, and also lead it in the closing set. The congregation usually learns a song

after the second time in a single worship service.
When I lead a new song twice in the same service, I usually won't do all the verses the first time around. I don't want to spend too much time in learning-a-new-song-mode. So, we'll just sing the first verse multiple times. The congregation learns the melody better without having to learn multiple verses. When we do the song again later in the service, the congregation has an easier time learning the other verses since they've sung the melody a few times already.

3. Teach the bridge. The bridge in many modern songs can differ greatly from the rest of the song, so you may want to take the time to teach it. Often the bridge contains multiple lines in a tune quite different from the rest of the song. However, often, the worship leader does not teach the bridge. They just sing it through once. I find that if I don't teach the bridge, people still don't know it by the third or fourth time we lead the song. (Although this may be changing over time with a new generation that has access to online libraries of digital music.) That's because unlike the verse and chorus, you might only sing the melody of the bridge once each time through the song.

In conclusion, consider how your congregation would benefit from you taking time to teach a new song. Your fellow worshipers will appreciate it, especially those who do not typically sing or play instruments. Teaching the song will enable the congregation to better focus on worshiping through that new song. Additionally, when you use that song again in the future, you've already helped congregation members to truly learn it and it will be easier for them to worship through that song.

WORKBOOK

Chapter Twenty-Five Questions

Your Heart: Describe a time when you encountered a new song at a worship service with no planned introduction or instruction. Was your worship hindered and how might the song have been presented in a way that made it easier to accept and learn?

_____

_____

_____

_____

_____

_____

_____

_____

Your Church: Are there songs that are familiar to one segment of your congregation but not another? (For example, hymns that a younger group may not know or contemporary songs that an older segment might not be familiar with.) How can you effectively introduce songs that are well known to only a portion of the congregation?

_____
_____
_____
_____
_____
_____
_____
_____
_____
_____
_____

Your Commitment: Practice teaching a new song to a small group, such as your family or a Bible study group. Get feedback on what helps them to learn it and notice how many times through it takes most people to pick up the song.

_____
_____
_____

Chapter Twenty-Five Notes

PART FOUR: LEADING

Chapter Twenty-Six:
Worship Cues for the Band

All bands use cues to communicate while playing from time to time. A cue can come in different forms: a glance, a hand signal, or a verbal cue. If you are prepared, you shouldn't need many cues. If you never deviate from a practiced arrangement, you won't need cues. But sometimes the situation or the Spirit seems to call for a change in the arrangement. In these cases, you need methods to communicate to the band that you are making a change.

If you practice with your music team and really understand each other, you will know when the leader wants to change an arrangement. You can feel it coming. And by the time the leader signals the change in the arrangement, the entire band (and, hopefully, slide operator) is ready to follow along.

But such musical tightness takes time and skill. For now, let me share some tips, even tricks, to help cue the band (and congregation) of a change of pace or direction.

How to Cue the Worship Team

To be able to cue the worship team effectively, keep these two aspects in mind:

1. Arrange the band so everyone can see the leader. It's important that the band members can see the leader, even if the arrangement appears awkward to the congregation. It might look nice to spread the band across a twenty-foot stage. But if the band needs to see the leader to musically stay tight, then bunch them together.

You could orient the band so that the leader, should he wish to, can see certain members of the band: the drummer, lead vocalists, the pastor (or presider).

The band member I usually want to see is the drummer. If I need to adjust the tempo, I need to direct the drummer since the percussion controls so much of the tempo. I often ask worship teams, "Who is the team leader?" They usually give the correct answer. But then I ask them, "Who is the musical leader?" and they look puzzled. Isn't is the same person as the team leader?

I don't believe so. The leader is the person with the most influence. The musical leader then is the person with the most musical influence on the team. In my view, the drums control the tempo and dynamics. It's the nature of the instrument. Drums are louder, keep a steady beat, and you can actually *feel* them when they play. If the tempo is off, then you need to make eye contact with the drummer so you can get back in sync. If you don't have drums, the musical leader is whoever controls the tempo and dynamics most. If you are leading with a piano accompanist, make no mistake: The pianist influences the tempo and rhythm more than you do with your voice.

The other team member I'd like to have eye contact with is a lead vocalist. I'll often have one of my female vocalists lead a song. (I do that for vocal variation from my male voice. Also, their voices are better than mine!) In my context, these are mostly Asian American sisters. In my experience, they tend to be less assertive, so they appreciate the affirming nod to assure them, "Yes. Start singing now."

The final person I want to have eye contact with is the team member offstage: the pastor. Now, in larger churches with huge stages, you usually can't see the pastor because they're too far away, or because they're behind stage, or because the stage lights blind you. But in most of our churches, the pastor is right there in the front pew, off to the side.

I want to be able to see the pastor for all sorts of reasons. Sometimes the pastor will want to cut the set short. Other times, the pastor wants me to sing that song again. Once, my pastor signaled me to give the closing prayer because he needed to leave immediately. Most of our churches don't have professional stage managers wearing walkie-talkies on their heads in their all-black outfits. The closest we get to stage direction is when the pastor points at his watch to signal, "We're late, and we've got to end now!"

2. *Exaggerate your movements.* If you're about to sing, really lift your head, open wide your mouth, and tilt your head back to give the cue. If you're about to end a song, step away from the microphone as you finish singing to signal the end of singing.

Guitarists have difficulty giving cues because they usually can't signal with their hands. I once saw worship leader Kevin Prosch lift his guitar neck higher to signal the close of a song. I have seen Tim Hughes lift his left foot behind him to tell his band to wrap up the song.

If the worship leader isn't holding an instrument, they'll often use hand signs. At Urbana 96, I watched the worship leader twirl her finger around to signal "keep going." Another leader made a "C" with her hand to signal chorus. She'd flash one, two, or three fingers behind her back to signal which verse. And she'd pat her head to say, "Back to the top." Such cues worked for her, though I find them a bit awkward and conspicuous.

I think the best cues for the band are the same cues we give to the congregation. After all, it's not like we want the band to know where we're going in the song and want to trick the rest of the congregation into singing something else.

How to Cue Your Congregation

There are four main aspects to cuing your congregation:

1. Cue them what to sing next. Say (or sing) the next line you'll sing before you sing it. If you've just sung verse one in a hymn, there's usually a few beats of interlude. During that time, tell them we're going to sing next sing verse two next. Or verse three. Or we're repeating verse one. But tell them before they need to know.

Usually, you should call out what to sing next a few beats before you sing it. If the next line we're going to sing is "'Twas grace that brought..." then say that. But don't say it if you're planning to insert another four bars of strumming the same chord. Otherwise, people will think you mean at the next downbeat. Wait to cue what to sing next until it's about time to sing.

If you cue people by calling out the first line of the verse, make sure the verses do not start with the same line. For example, the hymn called "Holy, Holy, Holy" by Reginald Heber has four verses.[12] But each verse begins with the same words, "Holy, holy, holy." So instead of calling out the first words of each verse, I usually call out the first distinguishing words. In this example, I would call out "All the saints" to introduce the second verse. The congregation and the person controlling the lyric slides will know that I mean the verse that begins, "Holy, holy, holy, all the saints adore Thee."

2. Cue the congregation when not to sing. You should cue the congregation when you don't want them to sing. Say you plan to insert an unexpected musical interlude with the voices at rest. If people are used to singing and not expecting a musical interlude, they will start singing unless you cue them otherwise.

Sometimes the worship team has prepared a musical offertory for the congregation to listen to (and not sing along). But if the screen shows the lyrics (because you didn't tell the slides operator not to project them) and you don't tell the congregation otherwise, they will start singing along. Most people won't notice it, but the worship leaders in the congregation will. I notice whenever this happens.

Now, if the worship leader invites the congregation to either sing along or simply listen, this is fine. But sometimes, the worship leader wants to invite the congregation to pause singing, rest their voices, and reflect upon the words. In such a case, the worship leader can offer a clarifying introduction to the song, such as "The worship team has prepared an offertory song, and we invite you to listen along in a spirit of worship and reflection."

There are several ways to cue not to sing. You can remove the lyrics from the screen. If the congregation sees the lyrics are removed, they will realize it's not time to sing.

Another technique I've used to cue when not to sing is to step away from my microphone. I do this in a way that is noticed by the congregation but not distracting. Most people know that if the lead singer is nowhere near the mic, he's not going to start singing. So, I step away from the mic for a longer-than-normal song intro. I step away from the mic when we have a longer musical interlude. And, I step away from the mic to signal that we've sung our last line of that song and the band is playing the ending.

3. Cue when you're changing a familiar arrangement. If a congregation is used to repeating a certain line or chorus but you want to change it up, you've got to cue them somehow. At certain times, it's not as smooth to say, "Now, at the end of the second time we sing the chorus, instead of repeating the chorus before the bridge—like we usually do—we're going to repeat the second verse again. Watch for my signal."

In such cases, it may be useful to offer a simple phrase like, "We're going to sing this song a bit differently today..."

4. Cue with body language. One Sunday I had to lead worship with a sore throat. I decided to exaggerate the mouth movements while singing quite softly. During the set, I realized I needed to cue the congregation, but my voice just wasn't up for it. So, I did the next best thing I could think of. I used a nonverbal cue.

I acted like I was going to sing. When it came to the time I would usually call out what to sing next, I used a silent motion instead. I tilted my head back, opened my mouth, and made as if I was going to sing. No words came out, but people got the cue. They started singing even though I did not. This became my most used nonverbal cue.

Congregants appreciate knowing when it's time to sing. And if the lead singer looks like he's opening his mouth to sing, then they'll do the same.

When to Use Cues

However you opt to cue your congregation during a set, remember the purpose for cues is to direct the worshipers (and the worship team) when what to sing or do next is unclear. Unnecessary cues are distracting.

If you plan to sing through all the verses of a hymn in order, most people assume they'll sing the verses consecutively. Don't give a cue. But if you decide to only sing the first, second, and fourth verses, then tell them and give them a cue after the second verse so they don't sing the third verse.

If you lead a song that everyone hears on their smart phones or the radio, then you probably don't need to cue anyone. That is, provided you use the same arrangement.

But if the song is less familiar to enough people in your congregation, then give a cue. How many is "enough people?" The answer depends on your context. In a congregation of fifty, if ten people don't know the song, that's twenty percent of the church. I would probably teach the song and give cues. But in a congregation of five hundred, if twenty people don't know the song, that's only 4 percent. I probably would not give cues unless we were singing it for the first or second time.

If you lead a familiar song with an unfamiliar arrangement, give cues. If you take a familiar song and change the tune, inform the congregation and give cues. A familiar song with an unfamiliar arrangement will feel like a new song to people.

If, for any song, you usually go straight from the first verse into the chorus, but this time want to repeat the verse, then cue the congregation. Otherwise, most people will just go into the chorus.

I hate to see a band work hard at coming up with a fresh arrangement, only to have the congregation barrel ahead into the old arrangement. In my context, this happens a lot with the song "I Could Sing of Your Love Forever."[13] The worship team planned to repeat the first verse, but the congregation went into the chorus because they were not properly cued.

Why does this matter? Well, in my context, in which people are already less confident in singing, they got "burned" by singing the "wrong" line. This made them even more hesitant and unsure about singing the next time. It also distracted people because, all of a sudden, people were singing different things. And finally, in that situation, I think people felt embarrassed for themselves and the worship team. All this distracted people from the point of the song and derailed their attention from worshiping God.

I realize that for many congregations, such an event may hardly be noticed. People may realize what had happened and continue singing unperturbed. If that's your situation, may I say you are blessed. But in most of my experiences (especially in Chinese-heritage churches), this kind of situation was quite distracting and actually discouraged our worship team.

Why We Cue

Even though we should focus on God during singing, people often watch the worship team to know what to do and when. Cues can ensure a worship set runs smoothly and with as few distractions as possible. The more a congregation is comfortable or familiar or skillful in music, the less the material in this chapter may be helpful. But for those leading worship in churches or cultures in which corporate singing is not a normal, common, or even accepted practice, learning how to lead in those situations may bless the congregation.

WORKBOOK

Chapter Twenty-Six Questions

Your Heart: Describe a time when your worship team or congregation started singing something other than what you had planned because you failed to give an appropriate cue. What sort of cues have worked effectively, and which ones have not?

_____
_____
_____
_____
_____
_____
_____
_____
_____

Your Church: Evaluate the setup on your platform. Are you able to see the musical leaders such as the drummer and the pianist? Can you see the pastor? Can each member of the team see you? If there are visual blocks, how can you eliminate them so that everyone can see the cues they need?

_____
_____
_____
_____
_____
_____
_____
_____
_____
_____

Your Commitment: With your worship team, plan and practice cues both for your own team and for the congregation.

_____
_____
_____
_____

Chapter Twenty-Six Notes

PART FOUR: LEADING

Chapter Twenty-Seven: Eyes—Open or Closed?

Should the worship leader's eyes be open or closed during worship? This question might surprise some. After all, shouldn't we open or close our eyes as the Spirit leads, or as the music plays? After all, most worshipers in the pew probably don't wonder, "Should I open or close my eyes now?"

Or do they?

If you've been reading through this book, you may have realized that the congregations I've led tend to be less musically expressive. They also include many people from unchurched backgrounds. Many people who have attended churches for a long time, or who just come from more musically expressive backgrounds, may not have even bothered to ask this question. So maybe the "regular worshiper" does not ask this question.

But you're not a regular worshiper. You're a worship leader. You would do well to think about it.

Regardless of whether you open or close your eyes, you are the leader. Therefore, you are also the example. So, if you often close your eyes, you model closing your eyes to block out distractions. If you keep your eyes open, you model as well. Like much of what I share in this book, there are both good and bad reasons to open or close your eyes. There are times when you should model closing your eyes to focus on God. And there are times when you should model keeping your eyes open during songs.

In some songs, it makes sense to close your eyes. These include songs in which we sing to God. These are songs that we speak in the first person to God. Where else would you look if you were saying "I love You, Lord?" At the back of the head in front of you? You might, but I suggest not.

In other songs, it doesn't make sense to have your eyes closed. Usually those are songs in which you are not singing to God. Lines like "You and I were made to worship"[14] or "Sing with me, how great is our God"[15] are meant to be sung to other worshipers. The medieval churches did this by constructing their churches in the shape of a cross so that church members could look at one another. (That practice of facing other worshipers while singing would make many today feel awkward, but it has merit.)

It also makes sense to open your eyes whenever you're singing a new song. You're teaching people the song, so show them how to sing. You can also watch them to see how well they learn the song.

If you're learning the song yourself, it makes sense to keep your eyes open so you can read the words. You won't believe how often someone closes their eyes while learning a new song, and then realize they have to open their eyes because they don't know the words. I see this regularly.

Like I mentioned above, besides all these reasons, some people do wonder if they should open or close their eyes. Some fear singing the wrong words. Some fear they might bump into their neighbor if they close their eyes.

Non-Christians and younger kids both have asked me, "Why do people close their eyes during worship?" While they're asking me that, they also say, "And what's with the hand lifting?" You may have heard other concerns.

So, remember to educate and serve all the congregation. I hope some in your church will be new to singing in worship services. I hope some in your church will ask about closing their eyes. I hope some in your church will not be longtime Christians. In other words, I hope you have nonbelievers and recent converts regularly visiting your services to hear the gospel.

Again, these are conversations that you should have with your team and pastor. Maybe not every week, but once in a while, raise the issue after a practice or in a meeting with your pastor. Chances are there's always someone in worship wondering, "Should I open or close my eyes?"

WORKBOOK

Chapter Twenty-Seven Questions

Your Heart: When you are worshiping but not leading, do you prefer to have your eyes open or closed or some combination? How does closing your eyes enhance your worship? When can it actually be a distraction?

_____
_____
_____
_____
_____
_____
_____
_____
_____
_____

Your Church: Look around on a typical Sunday morning and notice which songs cause worshippers to more readily close their eyes. What about these songs invites that response? Are there some worshippers who choose alternate eye positions, such as eyes turned upward or downcast, and what might these postures say about their worship experience?

_____
_____
_____
_____
_____
_____
_____
_____
_____
_____

Your Commitment: Look over your order of worship for this coming Sunday. Note which song(s) would be appropriate for having closed eyes and how you could model and (if necessary) explain to the congregation the benefits of this practice.

_____
_____
_____

Chapter Twenty-Seven Notes

PART FOUR: LEADING

Chapter Twenty-Eight: When Things Don't Go As Planned

No matter how much you plan, surprises can happen. There are certain factors that increase the chances of unexpected events interrupting our worship services. For example, if you are a smaller church that rents a building, like a school, and don't have your own keys to enter you may run into trouble. It could also cause problems if you have a smaller operation and a few overworked people are setting up the gear, running the video, and leading worship. Or perhaps your gear is comprised of "hand-me-down" equipment from another church.

In this chapter we talk about when things that don't go as planned. Here are some common problems I've encountered over the years, and how we struggled our way through them.

The gear isn't ready.
The words don't match.
There are no words.
The power goes out.
The people don't sing.

1. The gear isn't ready. This problem comes in many forms. A worship team member showed up late. The instruments aren't set up in time. We haven't performed a sound check yet. The sound system isn't ready.

These situations would be unacceptable on Broadway or in a megachurch. But in our small- to medium-sized ministries, they happen frequently. In most of our churches, a few people serve in multiple roles. We serve as roadies moving the gear, technicians setting up the gear, engineers running the gear, and musicians playing the gear. Not to mention, we comprise the cleanup and break-down crews as well. It happens: It's time for church to begin and the gear isn't ready. Sometimes, the gear isn't even there.

In those cases, I suggest you do the best with what you have. No drums? Fine. Play without drums. No time for sound check? It's not Broadway, so it will probably won't be the end of the world if we don't do a sound check. If you have to play songs with a different set of instruments, you will likely have to play the songs differently.

You don't like not having the full-time sound tech or the full PA system? Neither do I. But sometimes we have to make do when it's time for the worship service to begin. After the service, exercise due diligence to analyze the problem and propose solutions.

Remember, for almost two millennia, Christians did not have PA systems, yet they still worshiped fine.

2. The words don't match. Maybe a single word is misspelled. Maybe the worship slides have some mixed-up lines. Maybe the slides operator put up the incorrect lyrics. The point is, the words don't match.

The first step to tackle the problem of mismatched words, is to notice the error in the first place. Here we have another test of your attentiveness while leading worship. Many a worship leader won't notice that the projected lyrics were wrong. You can't remedy the problem if you don't know it's there.

You also don't have to do this alone. Consider inviting others to help you find any errors in the slides. Enlist people in the congregation to note errors and let you know so the errors can be fixed. Remind the slide operator to not just advance the slides but also to read along and focus to catch errors. Perhaps encourage the slide operator to attend worship practices from time to time. (See Chapter Thirty-Three.)

The scale of the remedy depends on the size of the problem. If it's just a word or two that's wrong, sing the song as normal and correct the mistake after the service, especially if it's a slide you won't be returning to. If it's a part of the song you *could* return to, such as repeating a verse, then you may want to consider skipping the repeat. If it's a part of the song you *must* return to, such as a chorus, then your response depends on how off the words are.

If it's just a word or two, chances are people can guess the correct word and fill it in. If people don't know what the words are, you can sing or say the line before you get there.

If the entire verse is wrong, then I suggest you mistrust the rest of the slides for that song and call out a repeat of the first verse. At least you know that verse is correct. If the problem is with the first verse, you may want to end the song soon.

Alternatively, the slide operator can go to a blank slide while they sort out and correct the issue.

3. There are no words (or the power went out). If you start leading the song and realize there are no slides for the song, then figure out a way to end the song with as much immediacy and grace as you can. But if it's because the power went out, then there are several things you can do. Again, the solution depends on the problem.

One time the power went out while I was leading worship. With God's help, I'm sure, I quickly thought of a song that both the band and congregation could sing without music. We had a great time singing. Eventually, the power outage forced us to vacate the building, so worship was cut short anyway.

4. The people aren't singing. If you are leading and there realize that people are not singing, you should probably figure out what's happening. If the congregation usually sings, you should check if the lyrics are even projected. Most likely, you started the song before the slides' operator could put up the song lyrics on the screen.

But if the words are there and the congregation isn't singing, you may want to check if something else is happening. A man in my congregation passed out during a song one week and collapsed forward into the next row. I saw the man crumple and I heard the wife scream. The only reason I noticed those two incidents was because I was watching the congregation. (Fortunately, I didn't need to watch my music or the band, and I sang with open eyes. See Chapter Twenty-Four.)

But had I missed those two signs, I would have undoubtedly noticed that a large swath of the congregation stopped singing and turned toward one direction. Imagine people's heads turning toward the same spot, like the ripples made when you drop pebble on a pond. That's what I saw, and the change in volume, demeanor, and the unexpected movement of the heads were like a neon sign flashing "Look here!"

In that case, I kept on leading and singing, and eventually, the whole congregation refocused. (Some kind folks helped that couple out of the sanctuary. I'm glad to report they were fine.)

Short-Term and Long-Term Solutions

In each of above examples, I shared some immediate remedies. But all these problems may point to deeper issues of training, commitment, and resources. There are long-term solutions that may need to be considered as well. The problem with long term solutions is that, well, they take a long time to fully implement. But you will better serve your worship ministry by implementing them in the long run.

Here are some examples for the different short-term and long-term solutions for various problems:

- *Not being set up on time for a service.* Short term solution: Skip the sound check and do your best. Long-term solution: Address unreliable equipment (or people).

- *Slides that are missing or are out of order.* Short term solution: Skip the verse or a song. Long-term solution: Arrive early and check the slides before the time for worship. Even modern software that synchronizes lyrics to song databases may have errors.

- *Typos or dropped words in a slide.* Short term solution: Smile and sing through the mistake. Long-term solution: Train your people to proofread and double-proofread the slides.

Consider creating a list like the one above of regular, common, or possible setbacks you may encounter in your worship service with a corresponding "action plan" for short- and long-term solutions for each of the problems. You may even consider providing this resource for everyone on the team, so you are all on the same page for how to respond to these hiccups, while also working toward long-term changes.

WORKBOOK

Chapter Twenty-Eight Questions

Your Heart: What is your response to interruptions and unexpected problems? Are you gracious or irritated, forgiving or angry? Which do you prize more: your image as a worship leader or the glory of God? How can problems in a worship service reveal character issues in your own heart that need to be addressed?

_____
_____
_____
_____
_____
_____
_____
_____
_____
_____

Your Church: Do those on your worship team have a shared commitment to excellence? Are problems and setbacks the result of unavoidable situations or a lack of commitment or concern? Is more training needed? Are more volunteers needed?

_____

_____

_____

_____

_____

_____

_____

_____

_____

Your Commitment: Are there problems that seem to be frequently reoccurring? For each of these, brainstorm a long-term solution that will address the root causes of the issue and make your short-term fix rarely needed.

_____

_____

_____

_____

_____

Chapter Twenty-Eight Notes

PART FOUR: LEADING

Chapter Twenty-Nine: Ask—Did Worship Go Well?

This may sound unspiritual, but as a leader you should ask, "How did worship go?" You should analyze how things went. That includes how the technical aspects went, such as the musical excellence, technical execution, etc. That also includes asking the spiritual aspects. Were people worshiping? If not, why not? If yes, then how engaged and sincere did they appear?

Watch the congregation. Were they expressive (relative to their culture, temperament, etc.)? Were they reverent when they should have been? Were they jubilant when they should have been? Did they smile when singing of God's beauty or kindness? Were their spirits and heads bowed when they sang of their brokenness? Were they responsive and engaged? Or were they staring into space, barely mouthing the words?

Growing as a Leader

Get feedback on your worship sets from other leaders, the congregation, and your pastor. Be open to change. Be prepared to get humbling feedback as well as encouragement.

Lead as often as you can. Like most skill sets, the more experience you gain, with the proper coaching, the more effective and efficient you'll become as a worship leader. Don't push out others who also desire to lead. But if possible, don't lead worship just once a month or less frequently. You will find it much easier to gain confidence and skill if you lead worship more than twelve times a year.

WORKBOOK

Chapter Twenty-Nine Questions

Your Heart: How can you have a heart of worship that is separate from your performance as a worship leader? Ask God to help you avoid basing your worth as a worshipper on how things go, but at the same time to continually learn and grow as a leader.

_____

_____

_____

_____

_____

_____

_____

_____

_____

Your Church: Take note of any time that a church member mentions that worship specifically ministered to them that day. If more than one member says something, or a member who rarely comments has something to say, pay extra close attention. What factors contributed to their overall feeling that it was a "good" worship service?

_____

_____

_____

_____

_____

_____

_____

_____

_____

_____

Your Commitment: Write out a bullet list of what a "good" worship service looks like at your current church with your current worship team and congregation. Are your expectations realistic? Now use this list to evaluate worship over the next few weeks. What trends do you notice and what do they reveal about the strengths and weaknesses of your services?

_____

_____

Chapter Twenty-Nine Notes

PART FOUR: LEADING

Chapter Thirty:
Pastors Versus Worship Leaders

Have you ever observed (or felt) tension between the pastor and the worship leader? This issue seems less pronounced these days as more worship leaders seek theological training and more pastors possess musical skills. But the tension persists in many churches.

The tension has to do with different priorities and expectations between the pastor and the worship leader. The pastor feels responsible for the worship service. The worship leader wants the music to be good. These goals appear to conflict at times.

My goal in this chapter is to help the worship leader understand the pastor's concerns and goals. I also hope pastors will gain insight into their worship leader.

Many pastors love music but lack musical training. Though they recognize areas in which worship leaders can improve, they might not know how to equip them. Sometimes pastors with limited musical ability feel intimidated or incompetent to give feedback on worship. Other times, pastors try to give advice that doesn't musically work. This frustrates both the pastor and the worship leader.

If you are such a pastor, accept your limitations to develop worship leaders musically. Seek out the most spiritually mature musicians and partner with them to develop worship leaders.

Many musicians have good intentions as leaders, but they find it hard to take advice about leading the worship from those less musically capable. They feel the pastor doesn't understand "the art." They get frustrated or discouraged when the pastor says, "The music is too loud," or "Can't we sing that a cappella?" or the dreaded "Please take out a song from the worship set because my sermon is too long."

If that's you, then understand that although your pastor may not be as musical as you, he probably does have important counsel on spiritual leadership. If you want to excel as a worship leader, then spiritual maturity is just as important—if not more so—than musical ability.

I encourage pastors and worship leaders to work together with grace and patience. I pray this book will be useful for your dialogue and mutual development.

WORKBOOK

Chapter Thirty Questions

Your Heart: What do you appreciate about your church's lead pastor? Do you pray for him regularly? Are you loyal to him (and do you encourage others to be as well) even when you may disagree with his decisions or preferences?

_____
_____
_____
_____
_____
_____
_____
_____
_____
_____
_____

Your Church: Describe a situation which you have observed or known about in which the pastor and worship leader were at odds with each other. In what ways does this damage a congregation? What Scriptures speak to the need for unity and what character qualities will be necessary to achieve it?

_____
_____
_____
_____
_____
_____
_____
_____
_____
_____

Your Commitment: Plan a time (such as an informal lunch) to talk with your lead pastor about his vision for your church's worship. Even if you have had such a conversation in the past, it is always a good idea to revisit the topic regularly. Be open to his feedback regarding what is going well and what needs improvement. Brainstorm ways that you can work together to improve the overall worship experience.

Chapter Thirty Notes

Part Five:
Notes

PART FIVE: NOTES

Chapter Thirty-One: Sample Letters for Church Leaders

Worship leader, have you ever read something and thought, "I wish my pastor (or someone else in your church leadership) understood this aspect of worship ministry?" Maybe, just maybe, the following notes will be useful for that purpose.

In this part of the book, I have included notes for different stakeholders in the worship music ministry: pastors, band members, instrumentalists, vocalists, and even the person running the slides with the song lyrics.

But before you hand this section to the person you have in mind, you should first check that what I wrote fits what you wish you could say to that individual. Feel free to personalize the letters, tweak them as necessary, or even use them as an example for writing your own letters.

Sometimes, it's easier for your stakeholders to critique the words of a "random author" than your own. Many times, I will bring in an outside speaker to address a topic. Because that speaker is an outsider who will likely never return, my church leaders usually feel free to disagree or critique what they've heard.

If I presented that same information, my leaders might feel less willing to disagree, or I might become defensive or take things too personally. So feel free to pass along any of these notes, and feel free to disagree with them! My hope is that these notes will help promote further dialogue with you and your worship ministry stakeholders.

WORKBOOK

Chapter Thirty-One Questions

Question: What are some things you want different members of your worship team or church leadership to understand about worship? What are some reoccurring issues that perhaps would be best addressed through a personal, heartfelt letter?

_____
_____
_____
_____
_____
_____
_____
_____
_____
_____

Question: Who on your team or in church leadership could benefit from hearing a bit about your perspective as the worship leader? Create a list of the different roles that you would like to communicate with.

_____

_____

_____

_____

_____

_____

_____

_____

_____

Action: Assess if it is necessary for you to use the following letters as a guide for writing your own letters to your team and church leaders.

Chapter Thirty-One Notes

PART FIVE: NOTES

Chapter Thirty-Two:
A Note for the Pastor

Dear Pastor,

 Your worship leader has given you this note because he wants you to understand a few things about the worship ministry. Maybe you already think about some of these issues. If so, thank you for working with your worship leader to encourage your congregation in acts of worship.
 I'm both a worship leader and a pastor who aims to build and strengthen bridges between these two vital roles in the church. Whether the following materials are a friendly reminder or first-time instruction, please hear the heart of your worship leader.

 Remember your role. First, as the pastor you are a more important and influential worship leader than he/she could ever be. Your worship leader may be on the stage for all to see, but people watch you to see how you engage in worship. Please remember that during our singing.
 During corporate singing, please join us. Please lead us. I know you sometimes need to go over your sermon

notes. You may want to make some last-minute changes to your message. You must do what you feel is right, of course. But if possible, sing with us. Worship with us.

Second, please give us feedback. The worship team wants to know your opinions about our ministry. We need to know your concerns and hopes for our worship ministry. If you really like something we do, please tell us. If you really can't stand something we do, please tell us—but please do so with love, humility, and sensitivity.

We hope you also will take our feedback. We love you. We want to support you. We'll even defend you if necessary. But we'd appreciate your asking us how we can improve the quality of our worship service, to the glory of God and for the building up of believers.

Third, worship is not second to preaching. But neither is preaching second to worship. Preaching is a part of worship. A church bulletin I read once listed all the elements of a worship service this way:

Worship through Prayer
Worship through Song
Worship through Scripture
Worship through Preaching
Worship through Offering
Worship through Benediction

This bulletin reminded me that all parts of the worship service should be, well, worship. It's a service of worship to God.

Don't blame the wrong person. Don't let people say, "We're experiencing technical difficulties," because they will automatically assume it's the fault of those working Audio-Visual (A/V). It might not be. It might be the worship team's fault because they didn't come early enough for a complete sound check. Don't blame "technical difficulties" if the pastor's mic has feedback, especially if the pastor wouldn't let the sound guy clip the mic as close to his mouth as he would have liked.

Be careful to not just tell the A/V folks that the sound was "too loud" or "too soft." It all depends on where you sit. If you're like most pastors in average-sized churches, you probably sit close to the front, and consequently, close to the speakers. In my church, I sit right in front of a four-foot speaker. At that range it *should* sound loud to me. If it doesn't, then I'm either wearing earplugs, or my hearing has deteriorated because I didn't wear earplugs. But it needs to sound that loud to me so the people in the back of the room can hear.

Finally, if you have slides for your sermons, please give your slides and cues to the slide operator ahead of time. Don't hand it to the slide operator on Sunday morning when you walk in. At that time, the slide operator is probably busy preparing for the worship service. If you can, provide the slides ahead of time.

Consider your comments about the music. Remember that to a worship team, comments about the music and sound are like comments about your preaching. We want the feedback, but we may also take it too personally sometimes. We crave encouragement, affirmation, and appreciation. You as a preacher appreciate someone giving you honest feedback, right? But you also probably like it when they do so in a loving way. Treat comments to the worship team about the music the same way.

Have you ever received suggestions about your preaching, but you knew that those suggestions were not helpful? Maybe it is because those suggestions were provided by someone who has never preached before and doesn't understand what's involved.

Well, unless you're both an experienced musician *and* an experienced worship leader, how do you think your comments about the music or the volume or the tempo sound to the band? Yes, we should all be humble and try to learn as much as we can from others. But let's be humble about how informed (or uninformed) our suggestions may be.

And if you have feedback about the music, especially negative feedback, consider holding it until later in the week. Most preachers I know don't want to hear critical feedback on Sunday just as they step down from the pulpit. They do want the input, though—even constructive criticism. But most preachers I know like to have some time between delivering the sermon and receiving negative comments. Same with worship leaders.

If you have critical feedback, maybe wait until later in the week. And when you do set up a time to give feedback, invite the worship leader to give you feedback as well. Just as you have feedback on the worship music, he'll have feedback on the preaching. Trust me on this.

Consider your song requests. If you have a song request, give it to the band as early as possible—preferably a couple of weeks before you want them to lead it. And if they say they can't do it or don't know the song, or they wouldn't lead the song unless you asked them, ponder those words.

Is it that hard to learn a new song? For some, no. For many, yes. The team will need time to learn the song. That involves multiple, time-consuming steps. They will have to find the song. They must get the correct lyrics (even if it's different from your version). They will need to check copyright or CCLI information. They will need to listen and learn the song. They will need to practice the song. They will need to type up the slides for the song. This translates into many hours per person. This doesn't take into account that the congregation might not know the song either, so the worship team will have to teach the song to the congregation before they can sing the song without distraction.

Please consider these factors carefully when you make special music requests. I trust your worship team is happy to honor your request. But that doesn't mean you don't count the cost before you ask them. Consider how much value that song adds to your worship service. Is it worth it? If it is, by all means, request it. You are the pastor, and you should do what you think is best for the flock. But if it's not worth it, or if you're not sure it's worth it, then have a conversation with your worship leader. Instead of a making a blanket request, figure it out together. Take it as another opportunity to work hand in hand with your worship team.

Offer your theological training and experience. Though you as a pastor might not have musical training, you probably have more theological training than the typical worship team member. This matters when evaluating song lyrics.

You may feel ill-equipped to comment on the music. But the worship team needs you to pastor them through a biblical evaluation of every song. Look at the songs before that Sunday. Don't wait until Sunday during the service to realize that the worship leader picked a song with bad lyrics, especially if he e-mailed you all the lyrics earlier in the week.

Listen to your worship team's needs. Do you often hear feedback when you're preaching? Does your A/V team complain or bemoan the sound equipment as too old or unreliable? Maybe they're just whining. If so, pray they can rise to the occasion. But maybe they have a point: The sound equipment might truly need servicing or replacing.

I encourage you to help your A/V folks get the gear they need. I trust you purchase commentaries or tools in the original languages to help you preach. Likewise, provide the proper tools to your worship ministry team. Usually sound equipment is the last thing people think to resource, but it's the first thing they realize is lacking.

Read more. If you found this note helpful or interesting, you might want to ask your worship leader about the rest of this book. This might be a great opportunity to talk ministry with your worship leader and encourage one another.

WORKBOOK

Chapter Thirty-Two Questions

Your Heart: Reading through this note and thinking through your relationship with your worship leader, how would you describe your interactions? Are you rivals or part of the same team? Has there been misunderstanding or an effort at unity? Do you regularly pray for the worship leader and ask him or her for feedback and to explain the worship team's needs? Do you offer your suggestions and directives by "speaking the truth in love"?

_____

_____

_____

_____

_____

_____

_____

_____

Your Commitment: Plan a time to talk intentionally with your worship leader this week about how you can work together as a team even more effectively. Jot down questions that you would like to ask and be sure to listen carefully to the answers. Ask if you can stop by the worship team's rehearsal this week (the worship leader will need to build that time into the schedule, so please be careful to keep it to the time agreed upon). Take a few moments to encourage the team and listen to their concerns, ideas, and dreams for worship at the church.

_____

_____

_____

_____

_____

_____

_____

_____

_____

Chapter Thirty-Two Notes

PART FIVE: NOTES

Chapter Thirty-Three:
A Note for the Slide Operator

Dear Slides Operator,

You may go by different names: PowerPoint person, lyrics controller—or my favorite, "the person doing the slides." Whatever your title, you are a vital part of the worship ministry.

Though many churches still have pews with hymnals, more and more churches have transitioned to lyrics projected onto screens. Maybe you project the Scripture reading. Maybe you also project prayer requests before the worship service. That's fine. What I want to address here is projecting lyrics for worship in song.

The following are a few points I think every slide operator in the typical American church should know about their role.

And to clarify what I mean by the "typical American church," I don't mean megachurches with the latest sound equipment. I mean the church of around 100 or 150 attendees, where the computer used for slides might even be your own personal laptop. And you might not have so-called worship software that specializes in projecting worship lyrics. You just use PowerPoint or whatever presentation software your computer came with.

Here are some points I'm eager to share with you.

You are leading worship. Your role might be projecting words onto a screen, but it's vital to keep the bigger picture in mind: Without you, people would not know what to sing. Without the lyrics, it's just a band performance. Because of the lyrics you project, God's truth goes forth in song and people can participate in worship together.

Grow in your skill. One of the biggest lies from the pit of hell goes something like this: Anybody can run the worship slides. This is so not true. So not true.

Anyone who has run slides before will tell you it can be a nerve-racking experience. Everyone in the entire church is looking at the lyrics you project. If you do a good job, no one notices. But when you make a mistake, everyone—and I mean everyone—sees. People turn their heads to look at the computer station as if to communicate, "You got the slides wrong!"

Sometimes you might not even realize the slides are wrong. But you begin to fear you've made a mistake when more and more heads turn toward you and you realize, "No one is singing. Ack! I'm projecting the wrong song!"

Projecting the lyrics at the right time is both an art and a science. Practice doing it. Ask for feedback, especially from the worship leader and the pastor.

Get to know the worship team. As with most working relationships, the better you know the people, the better you can work with them. You are less likely to think "that loud drummer" and more likely to think about your friend, John. Instead of that "difficult singer who just won't sing into the mic," it's your sister in Christ, Jane. The "loud drummer" and "difficult singer" are problems. But John and Jane are people, fellow believers, and friends. Maybe not close friends to you, but most certainly a brother or sister in Christ.

Drop by the team's practice. Not only should you get to know the worship team personally, you can get to know the team by observing rehearsals. This may be hard to do regularly, but I encourage you to visit your worship team's rehearsal at least once in a while. You can learn a lot.

Have you ever wondered why the worship leader waits until Saturday night to send you the lyrics to the songs for Sunday? Well, perhaps you realize that the worship team's rehearsals are Saturday mornings. And because the team hasn't rehearsed, the leader can't finalize the worship set. He can't send you the set because *he* doesn't know the set yet.

Have you ever wondered why the worship team seems to run late for sound checks? Well, now that you've seen them rehearse, you realize that they have to take public transportation everywhere. They have to lug a bass guitar and amp onto the public bus.

Learning more about the team and their practices isn't about making excuses for their shortcomings, but it can give you a perspective that helps you serve better with them.

Most A/V people don't think about their Sunday duties during the week. The people running the sound mixer don't fret on Friday, "Oh, I hope I can plug in the cables properly this week!" (If they do, it has nothing to do with their week. They just need more training.) But a worship team has to commit hours to practice as a team. That requires travel, transporting equipment, rehearsing, and then taking everything down and back home again. Band members may also have to practice their instruments or vocal parts on their own during the week.

Contrast that with most A/V teams. They don't practice during the week. Many don't even have to set up the sound system because it's built into the sanctuary. And if they do have to do any setup, they likely have a similar setup from week to week. Sure, there are some exceptions. On one Sunday there may be an extra vocalist, so you set up an extra mic and stand. Or on another Sunday they send you a new song, so you have to type up slides for that song. But other than that, you as the slide operator might not have as much to do during the week. You come in on Sundays, set up the system, run the system, and break down the system. And if you worship in a room with a built-in sound system, you don't even have to lay cable, move speakers, or set up mics. You just turn the master switch on.

So, you could benefit by learning about the work and responsibilities of the worship band. I say this not to excuse the band if they are late or unprepared. I'm also not saying that I think your job is easy compared to theirs, or that you don't work hard. I'm just saying that we can always gain more perspective from understanding what goes into different ministry roles. And we might gain more appreciation as well.

Get the slides right. Please, *please* get the slides right. Think of all the work that went into preparing for worship. The band rehearsed. You arrived early, set up, and did a sound check. Your brothers and sisters have spent hours honing their musical skills, practicing, and setting up their equipment before the service. You have asked the Holy Spirit to move our hearts to worship God. So many people have worked so hard to get everything ready for Sunday morning worship.

And then the projector shines up this line for all to see:

How Grate Is Our God.
Imagine your response if you saw this during an actual worship set. You might chuckle at that line. Or you might squirm because you typed it. Or you might feel disappointed because you hoped to focus people's attention on God. But if people saw this line on the screen during congregational singing, one thing is certain: People are not thinking about God's greatness, at least not when they first read it.

And while some might think a wrong lyric may be funny, I believe it is sad. Instead of focusing on God, we think, "I guess the spell-checker didn't catch that one..." or, "How embarrassing!" or, "Can't we get the lyrics right!"

Please, make sure people see that God is great, not grate. Double-check that people sing about the Morning Star, not the Mourning Star. Proofread so that we worship Jesus Christ, not that other fellow, Jesus Chris. And in my Chinese-heritage church, make sure we sing to the Lamb of God, not the Lam of God.

Let's also fix the capitalization. Sure, we can honor the tradition of the honorific *You.* But don't capitalize metaphors or descriptions. God is the Lord of everything, not the Lord of Everything. (Unless you're thinking of the town Everything, Massachusetts.) And yes, God is worthy, but it's not worthy to write Worthy God. He is the mighty God, not The Mighty God.

For years my church had a slide that said, "God is the Great I am," but the Bible calls God the "great I Am." Capitalize "Ancient of Days" because it's a title. But not "the living" God, which is just a description.

As a general rule, follow the official lyrics of the song as found in CCLI. But change it if it needs changing. When in doubt, go with how a current English Bible translation uses capitalization or consult a reference manual like *The Christian Writer's Manual of Style.* Capitalize titles like *Ancient of Days* (Daniel 7:9), *Alpha and Omega* (Revelation 1:8), *Prince of Peace* (Isaiah 9:6), *Son of God* (John 1:34), *Lamb of God* (John 1:36), *Lion of Judah* (Revelation 5:5), *Messiah*, and *Christ* (John 1:41). Leave in lowercase descriptors like "bread of life" (John 6:35), "good shepherd" (John 10:14), "holy one" (Revelation 3:7), and "beginning and the end" (Revelation 21:6).

Sometimes you may want to capitalize when the Bible does, such as direct address. But in general, go easy on the capitalization.

Another suggestion is to type the slides in all caps. This may be easier to read from a distance, especially in a sans serif font. But in general, I would try to avoid using all caps because that's not what we typically see in songs and normal writing.

More important than capitalization are correct words and spelling. For better is one day in the presence of the "lord" than a thousand "daze" elsewhere (Psalm 84:10).

Learn the songs. We expect the musicians to learn the songs well enough to do their jobs. Should not the same go for people projecting the lyrics?

If you don't know how a song goes, learn it. Look it up online. Listen to it. Read the lyrics. If you have twenty lines of lyrics but you don't know the song, how will you know where to insert breaks in the slides? We might break up a line in the chorus or include a line in the verse that's actually part of the bridge. The way to overcome this is simple but takes time. Learn the song. Listen to the song.

The more you know the song, the more you can also anticipate where the song leader will go. The more you know the song, the more you can accommodate changes when the leader decides to repeat a chorus or skip a verse.

Ask the worship leader for the song/music. Many worship leaders provide resources to their musicians when they prepare to lead a new song. Maybe they provide an audio file of the song. Or perhaps they include a link to a video online in which a worship team played the song. Maybe they don't do that for the worship team. In any case, when the worship leader sends you the lyrics for a new song, ask for a recording so you can also hear the song. Or search for a recording yourself.

Show the slides of new songs to the worship leader. If during the worship service you realize a slide for a new song contains mistakes, it's too late. Ideally, you would catch those beforehand. Do your utmost to avoid any typos or mistakes on the lyrics and slides.

As a worship leader myself, I apologize for all the times I sent the songs late, and forced the person doing my slides to work late Saturday night or early Sunday morning to type up slides.

Be flexible. The worship leader may change the order of the verses or skip a song entirely. Be aware that even the most well-laid plans require change some of the time.

As a worship leader myself, I apologize for not always being clear on what we're singing next. And thank you for trying to keep up. In all these areas, please offer suggestions to your worship leaders so you can continue to work better together.

Read more. If you found this note helpful or interesting, you might want to ask your worship leader about the rest of this book. This might be a great opportunity to talk ministry with your worship leader and encourage one another.

WORKBOOK

Chapter Thirty-Three Questions

Your Heart: Do you view your work running the slides as a true part of worship ministry or as just a job in the church? How can you become more involved in the worship ministry as a whole (note the ideas listed in this chapter) instead of segmenting your part as something entirely separate?

_____
_____
_____
_____
_____
_____
_____
_____

Your Commitment: Pick one of the points in this chapter to focus on over the next month. If there is an area where you already know you are weak, choose that one. If not, ask the worship leader which one you should most focus on. Since getting the slides right is so important in your ministry, be sure to prioritize that highly if you have not already. Consider asking a member of the congregation to help you with proofreading if that is not a strong point for you.

Chapter Thirty-Three Notes

PART FIVE: NOTES

Chapter Thirty-Four:
A Note for the Sound Person

Dear Sound Person,

Thank you for your service as a sound person in the worship ministry. As with all the other installments of "Notes" in this portion of the book, I begin with disclaimers.

If you, the sound person, are a professional, then you probably know way more than I could ever offer to you. So this note is more for those who aren't in the music or sound industry.

I am not a professional sound engineer, nor do I have a background in acoustics. (You can probably tell by how I use the highly technical label "sound person.") But I have served alongside professional sound engineers—people who have designed and run sound systems for professional concerts and theaters on Broadway and in Las Vegas. More to the point, I have some points for every sound person in the typical American church trying their best to run the sound board for their Christian community.

You are leading worship. Your role may be turning knobs or sliding faders on a sound console but keep the bigger picture in mind: Without you, people would not hear the worship team. The congregation could not hear the sermon. View your role with the significance it deserves. Don't let it get to your head, but don't take it too lightly either. By your service, people can sing to God and people can hear from God.

Get feedback about your mixing. No pun intended, but get feedback—the good kind! Work with the worship team and pastoral team about the sound. Chances are, none of them are professional musicians or sound engineers either. So, work together to create as good and clean a sound as you can.

Ask the people who sit near the speakers if it's too loud. Ask the people who sit far from the speakers if it's too quiet. If those near say it's too loud while those far say it's too quiet, you're probably about right. Whenever someone tells me the music is too loud or quiet, I usually ask them how close or far away from the speakers they are, and then suggest they consider sitting in different places in the room to see if the sound levels are better for them elsewhere.

Use fresh batteries. My first and most influential mentor about all matters related to sound mixing taught me to always use fresh batteries. The pastor may not ask this for his wireless mic. The worship leader may not insist this for his wireless mic. But wherever I go, I always request fresh batteries. If they don't have any, that's okay, because I always bring my own.

In professional theater, they always use fresh batteries. It's just not worth it for a mic or other device to fail during the event. If it's important enough for the entertainment industry, surely it's important enough for Christian ministry. Do we want to risk a wireless mic losing power during a wedding ceremony, or a funeral, or a sermon?

If you want to save a little money, invest in a good battery tester so you can tell when a used battery still has enough juice in it. Just know that when a typical battery tester indicates a battery's level is on the low end of green, that still may not be enough juice for a ninety-minute worship service. Don't take the risk. If your pastor has spent hours preparing to preach God's Word, and if your worship team has spent hours preparing to lead people in worship, then do them the honor of giving them fresh batteries for their tasks. They'll be grateful you did, and so will you.

Learn to wrap cable properly. There are good and bad ways to wrap cable. Bad way: Wrap the cable around your hand and elbow. The good way is too complicated to offer a tutorial here. Look online or ask someone in the industry how to properly wrap and store your gear.

Remember that in most cases, the gear you are using belongs to the church or ministry. It's not yours, but you should treat it like it is. That doesn't mean treat it harshly. Treat those cables like you spent your own money on them. Even the most inexpensive quality cables are $25 for about fifteen feet of cable. My church's least expensive cables start at $30. Our most expensive cables run $100 each; those are the fifty-foot speaker cables. They may not look it, but those cables (and mics and amps!) are very expensive. They are also delicate equipment, so learn how to handle them properly.

Read more. If you found this note helpful or interesting, you might want to ask your worship leader about the rest of this book. This might be a great opportunity to talk ministry with your worship leader and encourage one another.

WORKBOOK

Chapter Thirty-Four Questions

Your Heart: How can you better view your tasks as a ministry and as a part of leading worship? Do you feel unappreciated in your task, and if so, how can you become more engaged as a member of the worship team (such as through prayer, seeking feedback, etc.)?

_____
_____
_____
_____
_____
_____
_____
_____

Your Commitment: Choose one of the technical parts of your job to focus on for the next month. What is an area that frustrates you and how could you get better training in that area? Consider talking to the sound technician at a large church in the area (often this is a paid staff position) and ask for tips that will work on the equipment you have.

_____
_____
_____
_____
_____
_____
_____
_____
_____
_____

Chapter Thirty-Four Notes

PART FIVE: NOTES

Chapter Thirty-Five: A Note for the Vocalist

Dear Vocalist,

Let me clarify for whom I intended this chapter. I am addressing the vocalist in the worship team. Unless you're a professional singer, you probably don't think of yourself as a vocalist, but rather as a singer. You might not even think of yourself as a "singer" but as "someone who sings on the worship team." Chances are, you love to sing, and hopefully, you love to worship God, too. But your career isn't in professional music. This ministry is purely an act of service for you.

Now, let me clarify who I am. I am not a professional singer. I'm not a singing coach. And I've never had professional voice training. But I have led worship with professional singers. By "professional," I mean people who made their living as singers. I'm not qualified to give you training tips to improve your voice, but I do have experience in working with singers who are regular people. And I have learned a few things about how to help them to lead worship better.

You are a worship leader. I know, I know. You love to sing. You might not like to speak or pray publicly, or even pick worship songs. But if you're in the worship team, you are first and foremost serving as a worship leader.

By worship leader, I don't mean that you give directions as to when to start singing or which verse to sing next. I also don't mean to say that you lead the band or the worship team. You might, but that's not what I'm talking about here. By worship leader, I mean you have a responsibility and privilege to direct people to worship God.

You're a worship leader when you're on the stage and behind a microphone. But you're also a worship leader when you're driving in traffic or playing basketball. You're a worship leader when the music plays and after the music stops. Worship leaders lead people to worship God all the time. They're not just song leaders or music leaders. They're worship leaders. They don't just lead songs; they lead people. (You can read more about this in Chapter One, "Not Just a Music Team.")

That means you must be more than a decent singer. You must be a good witness for the God about whom you sing. Don't just sing. Lead worship with your life.

Help us set up. Most of our churches don't have large teams of sound engineers and technicians to set up our gear. In all the churches I've led, the worship team had to transport, set up, and break down their gear. You, a vocalist, can be a big help.

The band member with the hardest job of transporting and setting up gear is usually the drummer. If that's so, then the band member with the simplest job is the vocalist. (Maybe also the pianist if they don't have to set up an electric keyboard.) You don't need to set up an instrument, tune an instrument, or replace guitar strings. You need to warm up your instrument, but so does everybody else. Vocalists are ideal supporters in helping set up and break down worship gear.

Learn basic A/V. If you're going to help set up gear, you should know the basics about the gear. Vocalists who take time to learn the basics of setting up the audio-visual equipment can contribute so much to the team.
Learn to properly unwrap and wrap up cables. Learn to properly put down a monitor. Learn the proper distance and height of mic stands for your teammates. Learn to lay down cable efficiently. Learn to help the drummer set up his many drums. Learn the basics of setting up the sound mixer. Take the video projector out of its case and plug it in. At the very least, grab the music stands and take the instrument cases off the stage. If you're not sure what to do, ask how you can help! The rest of the team will thank you for it.

Learn how to sing into a microphone. Proper microphone technique may sound like a strange idea, but it's one of the worship team skills that all vocalists should learn. Without getting into the theory behind microphone placement, I suggest this: Position the microphone on the stand at a 45-degree angle. Adjust the height of the microphone so that you are singing into the round, ball-like part of the microphone. I suggest vocalists position the ball-like part of the microphone so that it's in front of your mouth when you stand up straight and face forward. You should not have to tilt your head up or down to sing into the mic.
And I suggest vocalists sing with their lips on the microphone. If you watch concerts or professional performers, you'll see that most of them have their lips touching the microphone. If the idea of touching your lips to the church microphone sounds unpleasant, consider buying a basic, but quality microphone for yourself. (The

Shure SM58 is the workhorse of the sound industry and a great all-around microphone.) After all, most of the other musicians have invested in their own musical gear, like instruments. Perhaps you would consider investing in your own microphone.

If you acquire your own microphone, make sure you label it, use a good carrying case, and take it with you when you leave. If someone asks you why you have your own microphone, tell them the truth: You sing with your lips on the mic and you don't want anyone else to get your germs. (Or for you to get anyone else's germs.)

While we're on the topic of singing into mics, here's another point.

Get used to hearing your voice in the sound system. Back when we had answering machines hooked up to telephones, people frequently commented how they hated the sound of their voices when they heard them played back. "Do I really sound like that?" was a common question that housemates asked each other. We still record our voices for our voice mail, but unlike answering machines, whose cheap speakers blasted our voices throughout the house, voice mail messages are only played back through telephone earpieces for just one ear to hear.

Most of us are not used to hearing recordings of our speech, let alone singing. So many worship team vocalists feel insecure about how they sound. This is especially true in smaller churches with amateur singers and the many, many churches that may not fully understand what a stage monitor is for.

For the record, a stage monitor is a sound speaker aimed not at the congregation, but at the band. They are necessary for the worship team to monitor their sound in order to sing and play well. Even the best musicians need to hear the lead singer, the lead instrument, and the other band members in order to stay in tempo or blend their sounds. And that's why you as a vocalist must sing loudly and clearly into the mic. So that the rest of the band can hear you and you can hear them.

Don't step back from the microphone when you hear your voice in the main speakers. Maintain a distance of no more than one inch between your lips and the microphone. And if that's too hard to do with your eyes closed, then put your lips on the microphone so you always know where the mic is. Alternatively, don't close your eyes.

Lead with your demeanor. Lead not just your voice, but also with your demeanor, body language, and facial expression. When you sing a song about the joy of the Lord, wouldn't it be appropriate to reflect that joy with your appearance? I gave the worship team leader an experiment that I will now share with you. If people were to look at your demeanor before you started the next song, would they be able to guess what the song is about? They should (to a certain extent), if your body language and facial expression matches the message of the song.

So, if the line of the next song is "Joyful, joyful, we adore Thee," can your demeanor look it? What if your demeanor does not appear to match the song? People will not take your direction seriously. Why should they sing sincerely when the worship leaders look insincere?

I am not suggesting that you force your outward appearance or manipulate an audience with your stage demeanor. My point is that you have rehearsed and should be ready to sing. Rehearse not just the music, but also the manner in which you will sing. If you've ever sung at a best friend's wedding, you didn't have to be told to smile and be happy. You probably were beaming all on your own. And if you've ever sung at a best friend's funeral, you didn't need anyone to tell you, "Remember, this is a funeral, so sing with dignity and proper respect for those grieving." You just did it.

The same goes for every worship song in every worship service in which you'll ever sing. If the songs that morning are about repentance and brokenness, you should prepare mentally and emotionally to get into that mind-set. And if you are in that mind-set, chances are your demeanor will match that. And if your demeanor matches the song, your congregation will more likely follow.

Of all the band members, your demeanor as a vocalist is most important next to the worship team leader. Unlike the drummer who may be off to the side or in the back row of the stage, you are usually front and visible. Unlike the bass player who is hunched over his instrument, you are the freest of the band. Let your voice and expression support the team leader and the song that you are leading.

Don't just sing. Lead.

Read more. If you found this note helpful or interesting, you might want to ask your worship leader about the rest of this book. This might be a great opportunity to talk ministry with your worship leader and encourage one another.

WORKBOOK

Chapter Thirty-Five Questions

Your Heart: Are there areas where self-consciousness has hindered your ministry, such as not seeing yourself as a worship leader, being "afraid" of the mic or the sound of your own voice, or not expressing an animated demeanor for a song? Evaluate how self-consciousness may be limiting your ministry and how a renewed focus on God and others can help in overcoming embarrassment, shyness, or awkwardness.

_____
_____
_____
_____
_____
_____
_____
_____

Your Commitment: Commit to being a team player with the worship team. How and who will you help with set up and A/V needs? How will you encourage the other vocalists and team members?

_____

_____

_____

_____

_____

_____

_____

_____

_____

_____

Chapter Thirty-Five Notes

PART FIVE: NOTES

Chapter Thirty-Six:
A Note for the Drummer, Percussionist, and Bassist

Dear Drummer, Percussionist, and Bassist,

You might ask why I lumped you band members together. It's not because of some grouping by musical instrument. I write to you all because what little I have to say is the same for all of you. So, I thought I'd save everyone time and paper by combining these. If you play the drum kit, the shaker, the djembe, the triangle, or the electric or upright bass, this is for you. And for convenience, I'm going to lump drummers and hand percussion players together into the group "drummer."

As with the other "Notes" in this portion of the book, I offer my usual disclaimers: I'm not a professional musician. I'm not a music instructor. And among the typical band instruments, I am the least proficient at your instruments—especially the drums. But I have played worship with professional percussionists and bassists. And I would share my thoughts for the typical church percussionist or bassist in order to help them better lead worship.

You are rare. In the typical American church with fewer than 150 people, there are probably no drummers or bass guitarists. This is especially true of Asian American churches, and specifically of Chinese-heritage churches! If you're a musician in such a church, know that you are rare.

I have no statistics to back this up, just experience. That doesn't mean no one can play a serviceable bass. It also doesn't mean no one in the church can keep a decent beat with a kick, snare, and hi-hat. It just means that more people in our churches took lessons for classical piano and violin than for guitar, drums, or bass guitar. And in most Asian American churches, the kids get plenty of hours practicing classical piano and violin.

Like most of the other band members in typical American churches, you are not a professional, nor do you claim to be. I hope you enjoy playing your instrument in church, but I also know that drummers especially are compelled to play for worship because they're the only drummer in the church! I hope that you not only enjoy your instrument, but that you also love to worship God. And I especially hope that you not only love to worship God, but that you love God. Which leads to my next point.

You are a worship leader. You're not just a musician who leads music. You must be a worship leader who leads people. I say that because in my experience, especially in Chinese/Asian American churches and groups, I find a non-Christian pressed into worship team service. Oh, the non-Christian may be a swell guy or gal. (Maybe you are such a non-Christian serving on worship team.) The person may be dating or even married to a church leader. But since your instruments are one of the hardest-to-find in most of our (Asian) churches, I give you this warning: You are not just playing drums or bass; you are leading worship.

If your job was just leading music, then only musical qualifications matter. But since worship leading also involves spiritual leadership, spiritual qualifications also matter. (For more on this, see Chapter One, titled "Not Just a Music Team.")

Lead with your demeanor. In my experience, the drummer and bass guitarist usually have the bad reputation among the band in terms of engagement in worship. During the 1990s, when many churches were beginning to transition from organ/piano to worship teams, critics aimed their strongest objections at those two instruments. Percussion was inappropriate, loud, and disrespectful. The bass guitar was also too loud and boomy. Both of these instruments were associated with rebellion and edgy pop culture. But often, the strongest criticism from worshipers was about how the drummer and bass player didn't *look* like they were worshiping.

Because a vocalist has to sing the words of the song, he/she appears engaged in worship. But when congregation members looked at the drummer or bassist—and look they did—those people usually had frowns or stern expressions. The bass player and the drummer didn't appear to be worshiping. They definitely weren't singing either. They appeared to be just jamming.

When these criticisms reached me as the worship team leader (and vocalist and guitarist), I wondered why I wasn't concerned. I realized that I knew those individuals personally, and I knew them to be sincere Christians. I also understood that those musicians had to concentrate. Often drummers and bass players don't sing because the rhythms they play don't make it easy to sing along to the melody. I understood these things, but the older Christians usually did not.

So, when I sat in the pew and worshiped in church, I

paid more attention to those band members. Sure enough, while the vocalists often had smiles, the drummer and bassist looked stern, almost angry. When the worship leader told us to close our eyes during the next song, those musicians often kept their eyes open, even during prayer. Since I knew these musicians personally, I knew their intentions were noble. But I had to admit, if I didn't know better, I would think these musicians were not worshiping.

It didn't help that often the drummer and bassist didn't dress up as much as the others. Maybe vocalists feel more exposed or visible. After all, they stand at the front of the stage and their only cover is a mic stand. But the bass player seemed to be in his own world, sitting on a bass amp, head bowed over, as he grooved in his jeans. And the drummer, that guy wasn't even wearing long pants! He often wore shorts.

Again, I knew that the bass guitar is heavy, and sitting down helps conserve energy during a long worship set. Plus, most bassists practice at home in a sitting position, so it's only natural they prefer to sit onstage. I also knew that drummers have to move their legs to work the pedals. They already broke a sweat setting up the drum kit, and now they had to undergo rigorous calisthenics the entire set.

But I had to admit again that, if I didn't know better, the drummer and bassist looked like rebels: the holdovers from a rock-and-roll band invading God's sacred worship so they could be the center of attention in virtue of their loud and ostentatious instruments. So, we had to address this.

Deal with the image. Sorry if this is harsh. In most churches, especially ones who have been around during the time when hymnals were the main worship resource, folks still remember the days when the worship team consisted of the person in front holding a hymnal in one hand

and conducting (sort of) the congregation with the other. Unless you're at a younger church, you would do well to understand this recent history. The idea of drums and electric guitars in typical American evangelical churches really is quite recent: it started with the "Jesus People" in the Sixties and Seventies and then moved into more mainstream evangelical churches in the Eighties, beginning with churches like Calvary Chapel and Vineyard. Many of our older Christians still remember those earlier days fondly. And we should be aware of that and respond accordingly.

For their sake, do your best to look clean cut. Submit to your leaders and go the additional mile of asking them before you get a mohawk or dye your hair bright purple. One of my drummers, who is an excellent musician, came to me one day while I was still the team leader. He asked me if it would be okay if he came to church on Sunday with a mohawk. A real mohawk, the kind where a tuft of hair like uncut grass bisected an otherwise bare, razor-shaved head. Of course, there's nothing in the Bible forbidding a mohawk. But then again, I've got pretty conservative people in my congregation, and those are the people in their twenties and thirties. As for the people over fifty—would they even come back?

I tried to balance the liberty we have as Christians with the principle that we are servants to the congregation. I asked him why he wanted a mohawk, and he gave me what seemed like a reason anyone would give to get a new hairstyle. There was nothing rebellious or punkish about his desire, but I wanted to protect him and the worship team from any unnecessary misunderstanding.

I eventually told him, sure, but on that day, he would have to particularly dress up. I also put him in the back row that Sunday morning. Sure enough, someone asked me about it afterward. It was my senior pastor. He was okay with it, but he did ask me if I had thought about how others would perceive it. I admire my senior pastor for his openness, his honesty, and his concern for others. But aside from the two of us, I had no other conversations about that issue. The mohawk grew out in a few weeks, and we all moved on.

I suppose we will always have to manage this tension between congregational expectations and individual expression. I don't want my team members to just do or wear whatever they want, but I also don't want them to be afraid of how they think others will perceive them or to feel like they can't express themselves or their concerns. I pray for honest, trusting, loving team relationships.

I have no doubt that if I told this brother "no" about his mohawk, he would have humbly obliged. And to my drummer's credit, he asked me afterward if there were any issues about his hair. I cannot think of a humbler approach to our age-diverse congregation than what this young worship leader showed here.

But this incident was not in isolation. By that time, the worship ministry had established trust with the congregation. The worship team usually dressed in a manner that indicated that we took our roles seriously and with respect. So, if one Sunday out of many years one of my drummers sported a mohawk, no issue came from it. At least, none that I'm aware of.

Play music appropriate for the congregation. By this I mean, don't play a mind-numbing, awesome groove and back beat at full volume in a church of fifteen people. Unless they all love heavy metal, that probably won't work. Some songs were written for big, full bands in large gatherings. Other songs were written for when only few are gathered. Some songs can work in both large and small groups, but you should arrange them accordingly.

If your team leader asks you to play just like they did on the recording, consider how well that works in your situation. Many modern worship albums are recorded live in huge worship-concerts. Most of our churches aren't as large, so the singing won't be as loud. Plus, most of those worship concerts are filled with young people about the same age. But most of our established churches have multiple generations in the seats.

This may mean you can't play as loudly as you think you should. Does it drive you crazy when someone, especially the pastor, asks you if you can "just play a bit softer"? Yes, most of these folks don't realize that the quality of your tone changes with volume, especially for percussion. Hitting the drumhead for a softer volume also changes the feel of that sound. Maybe they don't know that. Still, you are first and foremost a servant. If they want softer, please find a way to oblige.

If you oblige them and build a reputation of servanthood and trust, things will change over time. They'll get used to drums. They'll even miss the drums when they're not up one Sunday. Drums and bass are a part of the modern musical landscape. The time will come in most churches when such instruments will not be an issue. (Perhaps in most churches, that time has already come. But maybe in your church, that time has not yet come.)

But if you make people feel ignored, act stubborn, and play as you see fit, the opposite will happen. They will run you off the stage and eventually, off the worship team. You must earn their trust. You must be a servant. You must recognize that the privilege is not they get to hear you play, but that you get to play for them.

Keep the beat. What I ask from my drummer and bassist is this: Keep the beat. I don't need fancy, and I don't want fanfare. If you can do fancy, that's fine. But most of the time, I need just enough beat to woo the congregation into the song's message and music. But more important than all that is for the rhythm instruments to keep the beat.

If you're an accomplished musician, then you already do this. But if you're newer to these instruments, then it may serve you to focus on a few key things, like keep the beat.

Read more. If you found this note helpful or interesting, you might want to ask your worship leader about the rest of this book. This might be a great opportunity to talk ministry with your worship leader and encourage one another.

WORKBOOK

Chapter Thirty-Six Questions

Your Heart: Why is a servant's spirit especially important for a drummer in the environment of many churches? What is your church's attitude toward drums and if there is opposition, what are some practical ways to patiently help to overcome negative perceptions?

_____
_____
_____
_____
_____
_____
_____
_____
_____
_____

Your Commitment: Have a friend video record you during a worship service so that you can study your demeanor. Are there ways that you can appear more engaged in worship while still keeping your focus (and keeping the beat!)? Work on how you will be a worship leader with the specific challenges you face.

Chapter Thirty-Six Notes

PART FIVE: NOTES

Chapter Thirty-Seven:
A Note for the Guitarist

Dear Guitarist,

Among all the instruments and the roles on worship team, I am most familiar with the role of guitarist, especially the guitarist who leads and sings. Though I am most comfortable in this role, I give the same disclaimers I've offered in my other "Notes": I am not a professional guitar player, nor am I an experienced music instructor. But I have logged thousands of hours leading worship and talking with pastors and worship leaders about the craft, and I have tried to apply the biblical principles of leadership and servanthood to this ministry. I'd like to offer a few things for you to consider as part of the worship team in your church.

You are a worship leader. Rarely is the guitar player anyone but a committed Christian, especially the leader. But that does happen, especially in one of two cases. First, if the ministry is very, very small, people might press a spiritually unqualified guitarist into service. Second, if the guitar player is very, very good, people might overlook a lack of spiritual qualifications and press the guitarist into service. In those situations, and some others, we find this: a guitar player who is not spiritually qualified to lead worship.

If the job was just leading music, then musical skills would be the most important qualifications. But this job is more about leading people, specifically leading people in worship. This is a spiritual activity. Thus, spiritual qualifications matter.

Lead with your demeanor, not just your music. I have said this to everybody else, and I believe it's worth saying again. Your facial expression, your body language, and your overall demeanor should match the song. As the guitarist, you still have a responsibility to model engagement in worship.

Unlike bassists and drummers, it's much easier to sing along with the song while playing guitar—more so playing rhythm guitar than electric. One way to model worship on guitar is to sing the song. Sing, even if there isn't a mic in front of you, like when you are not on stage but worshiping among the congregation. If you want the congregation to participate in worship, then you should model that.

Help other band members set up and break down. In the Chapter Thirty-Five, I urged them to come to rehearsals and services ready to help set up and break down worship gear. After all, most vocalists don't have equipment to set up, except maybe for their own mic and stand. But guitar players, especially acoustic ones, do have to set up. They have to carry their instruments, usually large and bulky. Then they have to tune their guitars. All this creates a sense that the guitarist has spent much time setting up.

But I find most guitarists can set up quickly. They can

tune their instrument in under a minute. And they don't need to warm up their fingers as much. And breaking down is even faster. All most guitarists have to do is put the instrument back in its case. So, while a typical acoustic guitarist does need a bit of time to set up and break down, it's pretty fast.

Here's what I don't want you to do, but sadly I see this more than I would like: The guitar player is playing his/her instrument while the rest of the team is still setting up or breaking down (especially the drummer or any electric instruments). At the end of a practice, the drummer starts the lengthy process of putting all the gear away. He does this because he knows it will take time. So as the drummer works away and collapses each stand, stores each cymbal, and moves each drum, the guitar player is still strumming. Why? Because he knows it only takes him a few seconds to break his stuff down.

As a guitar player, you need less time to set up or break down; do it sooner rather than later so you can help the others on your team. This goes back to what I said in the Chapter Five. Serve your teammates by putting your guitar back in the case straightaway, and then go and help break down the drums or wrap up cables.

Strum clean and in tempo. Fancy strums are the norm these days. As I've written already, the guitarist in the Eighties and Nineties only needed three or four chords to play most of the current worship songs. But today, things are different. Guitarists want to play like the recording with the same intro riff or solo they hear on the internet or radio. But for every hour a guitar player practices getting that one riff right for that one song, I recommend a better use of that time: Get your strums down clean and tight. And learn to stay in tempo. I would rather you play all your basic strums perfectly and forgo a fancy guitar intro, than play the intro perfectly but mess up the tempo.

In corporate worship, the fundamentals matter more. A clean strum and consistent tempo will enhance worship far more than a fancy guitar lick for one song.

Don't make everybody wait and watch you adjust your capo. I mentioned this earlier in the section on leading, but I want to repeat myself here because it's that common—and in case you hadn't read that chapter.

Many a guitarist will play to the end of the song, pause in silence to adjust their capo, and then resume leading. It's as if they think that the congregation and team are paused while they adjust their capo. Have you seen this? Have you done this?

Let me share a secret: we, the rest of the congregation, are not paused. We are waiting. And we're probably watching you. And if we don't play guitar, we don't even know that the doohickey you're fiddling with is called a capo.

Do you really want all attention fixed on your capo? Is there any other way you can make use of this time for a more immediate worship of God? Can you at the very least pray and adjust your capo? (Only do this if you can pray naturally.) Could you ask us to meditate on the lyrics of the next song? Could you ask another instrument to intro the next song? Any of these things are better than us watching you adjust your capo in silence.

Don't try to talk while strumming. In an effort to say a few helpful words, worship-leading guitarists will talk in between songs. Maybe they'll even offer a prayer. But in an effort to have a smooth flow between the songs, they will try to talk as they strum. Most guitar players sound like this when they try to strum and talk/pray at the same time:

"Father God..." (pause to change chord) "...Father, You are so good..." (pause to change chord) "...and we want..." (pause to change chord) "...we want to praise You..." (pause to change chord) "...we want to praise You because You are so good."

I do not exaggerate. Many a guitar play thinks he is speaking smooth, unbroken English. But when they are forced to listen to the recording afterward, they realize what they're doing. They have divided their attention between their instrument and their speaking. And they inserted an unnatural pause every time they changed a chord. And they changed chords every measure or two. This gets old. Fast.

I advise you to learn to pray/speak naturally while strumming (or playing the keys). Learn to pray/speak so naturally while playing your instrument that your speech sounds as if you're not playing an instrument at all. To achieve this, most people have to practice. Practice strumming and praying at the same time.

This is harder than it looks for most people.

One reason this is so difficult is that the in-between strumming differs depending on what songs you are in between. There's no go-to strum pattern you can use in between every pair of songs. So, you can't really simulate or practice this.

Another reason is that you should speak with measured words. After all, you're speaking before the Lord and His people. You're taking up time in the worship service. Every word and every moment we use during a worship service should add value and contribute toward the purpose of glorifying God. Too many people have not prepared what they want to say. I'm not saying you should memorize scripted prayers, although there's nothing wrong with that. I am saying that when you have to divide your attention between smooth playing and meaningful praying, you will usually end up doing neither.

So perhaps it's best if you don't try to play and pray at the same time. If you want to pray with music playing, ask another instrumentalist. Most guitar players can ask the keyboard player to vamp on the chords of the last song, or transition to the music of the next song. That gets the best of both worlds—appropriate music with sensible speech.

Read more. If you found this note helpful or interesting, you might want to ask your worship leader or pastor about the rest of this book. This might be a great opportunity to talk about ministry and encourage one another.

WORKBOOK

Chapter Thirty-Seven Questions

Your Heart: Is your heart to serve or to show off with your music? How do you know? When evaluating how to spend your practice time, ask yourself: "What will best serve my brothers and sisters in worship?"

_____
_____
_____
_____
_____
_____
_____
_____
_____
_____
_____

Your Commitment: Practice/plan for pauses. Are you able to play and pray at the same time? If this will require much practice on your part, do not attempt it until you are very comfortable doing so. What will fill the silence while you adjust your capo? Are you more focused on intro riffs or perfecting your strums? Become proficient at all your basics before trying out newer and fancier work with your playing.

_____

_____

_____

_____

_____

_____

_____

_____

_____

_____

Chapter Thirty-Seven Notes

PART FIVE: NOTES

Chapter Thirty-Eight:
A Note for the Band Leader

Dear Band Leader,

Hi again. Did you think all these notes at the end of the book were only for the others? I know we've covered a lot already, but the following points didn't seem to fit well in any other part of the book. So, I put them together here for you.

Work on your voice as much as your instrument. People who lead on guitar or keyboard or another instrument often fall into this same trap. They neglect their primary tool and worship-leading instrument: the voice.

I have seen worship leaders develop their skills on their musical instrument over years. They play cleaner. They increase in confidence. They can play complicated, even fancy music. But those same leaders don't improve at all in their singing.

You spent hundreds of hours honing your instrument skills, but how many hours have you invested in honing your singing skills?

Get a vocal coach. Take singing lessons at the local community college or adult school. Develop your voice. You've got a clean strum. You play beautiful notes. So why not sing with the best voice you can? Yes, we are all limited by the physical construction of our windpipes, mouths, nasal passages, etc. But chances are, you will hear appreciable improvement with diligent investment in improving your voice.

I don't think I have a great voice. But I have received a fair share of compliments about my singing. Just like I try to work on some technical aspect of my instrument every time I play it, I try to work on some technical aspect of my singing every time I sing. I practice singing in harmony, singing with fewer breaths, singing to blend in better with other voices.

My other tip is to invest in a quality microphone. Assuming your other components can match it, a pro-level quality microphone helps. My mic's quality is truly double that of the other mics. So, it's not surprising that my voice sounds warmer. But to get the most out of quality gear, you've got to have a quality sound system and people who know what they're doing.

Learn to recognize your default tempo. That's the tempo you naturally and gradually shift to for every song. Most worship leaders have one tempo. Whether they start a song faster or slower, by the time the second verse happens, and definitely by the bridge, they have reverted to their default tempo. And they are often completely unaware of it.

While most musicians have one default tempo, some of them have two default tempos: fast and slow. All fast songs have the same fast tempo. All slow songs have the same slow tempo. Most leaders slide back to their default tempo, but a decent number can maintain two distinct tempos. While the ability to play at two tempos is better

than just one tempo, this still limits our music.
Revel in and practice in the "middle" tempos. Feel the difference between 50 bpm and 66 bpm. Even if your congregation might not notice the difference, the music will feel different. Practice playing the same song at different tempos with a metronome. Or you can use my secret technique to stay in tempo: Make the drummer practice staying in tempo, and then follow the drummer!

I don't mean to imply that the leader who reverts to one default tempo is a poor musician. One of the best musicians I know, who majored in music in college, still falls prey to this tendency. This brother would eventually make every song the same tempo. By learning to play with a variety or rhythms and tempos, you create a musical program that is rich in tones and patterns that prevents worshipers from losing interest, becoming distracted, or feeling as if they're singing the same thing over and over again.

Let other instruments and voices start songs. As a rule of thumb, have at least one song in your set that starts with another instrument or voice besides your own. This gives sonic variety, and also makes more use of the skills of your teammates.

This is especially helpful in the flow from one song to another. Like a good DJ that starts the next song just as the current one stops, you can transition smoothly between two songs. I'll often close a song accompanied by just one instrument, say my guitar. I instruct my team beforehand that while I'm strumming the final bars of one song, they should be getting ready to start the next song.

Often the leader will start each song the same way. That's understandable. If the band leader plays guitar, then they'll naturally start songs with their strum. But for variety's sake, and to let other instruments take the lead, don't start every song with two bars of strumming. Let others start.

Lead with your demeanor, not just your music. I have said this to everybody else, and I believe it's worth saying again. Your facial expression, your body language, and your overall demeanor should match the song. As the principal leader and vocalist, you must model this and remind the team constantly that their demeanor leads the demeanor of the church.

Check the slides. I urge you to read all the notes for the band. I especially urge you to read the note for the person doing the worship slides. Hear me now: The worship slides are your responsibility. Let me say that again: The worship slides are your responsibility.

At least, their content should be. You might not type or prepare the slides. You might not operate the slides. But you must take responsibility to ensure there are no mistakes in the slides.

Think of all the preparation to lead worship. You rehearsed with your team. You arrived early, set up, and warmed up. You have spent hours practicing your instrument and your singing. You spent hundreds or thousands of dollars on your equipment. You have prayed that the Holy Spirit will move the church to worship God.

And then you read this line: *How Grate Is Our God.*

May it never be so!

What can you do to ensure the slides are correct? Ask for the slides operator to send you a copy of the slides before Sunday. Or, show up earlier on Sunday morning and check all the slides personally before the service begins.

It's too easy to blame the person doing the slides. Instead, encourage them. Come alongside them. Thank them. Help them improve. Don't do this in a condescending way. But do approach this with a sense of due diligence. Above all, do it with love and gratitude; without the slide operators, we could not lift our voices to God in unison.

WORKBOOK

Chapter Thirty-Eight Questions

Your Heart: Are you committed to seeing yourself as a worship leader? What does your demeanor communicate about your love for God and your worship through the songs?

_____
_____
_____
_____
_____
_____
_____
_____
_____
_____

Your Commitment: Pick one of these practical areas to work on: vocal training, default tempo, letting others start songs, or checking the slides. What will you do this month to pursue excellence in this area with renewed focus?

_____
_____
_____
_____
_____
_____
_____
_____
_____
_____

Chapter Thirty-Eight Notes

PART FIVE: NOTES

Chapter Thirty-Nine:
A Note for the Worship Team

Dear Worship Team,

I have points for the entire band and ministry team that I have not said yet because they didn't seem to fit in other parts of the book. These are not rules, but they are suggestions that I believe will help bring unity and cohesion to your ministry.

Proper attire. Dress appropriately for the worship service. Take your cue from the worship team leader. Even better, take your cue from the pastor. I find it a common but surreal occurrence when, in a worship service, the band is dressed casually or maybe even "smart casual" while the pastor has donned a suit and tie. This happens frequently, I think, because the pastor may be older and more traditional, but the worship team members are younger.

If you're in that situation, try to bridge that fashion gap as much as you can. I don't suggest that because your pastor wears a suit, you the drummer or bass player should wear a suit while the rest of the band is in jeans. But discuss it with the rest of the team. What kind of message do you send if the young, hip worship team dresses in dark jeans and graphic tees while the pastor-teacher wears a suit?

If you are in doubt as to how casual or formal to dress, I suggest you lean toward more formal, or what we just call dress "nicer." Why? There are those who say God deserves our best, so we should dress up on Sundays. There are also those who say God invites sinners to come and not be hindered by how well they dress. Some cite the parable where people came to a wedding feast dressed improperly and were thrown out. Others cite the passage about showing no favoritism between those dressed in rich clothes versus poor clothes. The point is to dress appropriately for your situation.

Maybe you are working the sound or lights and have to do the heavy lifting. Dress accordingly. Consider how you reflect your church or fellowship with your attire, not for the sake of legalism, but out of love.

Honest feedback. Musical tastes and standards vary. Criticisms about your music cut close to the heart because music can be so personal. Someone saying they don't like your voice is very different from someone saying they don't like the outfit you're wearing. If someone doesn't like your voice, it feels like they don't like your face.

But honest feedback must win the day. You expect the preachers to receive feedback and grow. You trust that the children's workers get screened. That's well and good. You also have high standards for the worship and music ministry. The pathway to excellence goes through the thorny brambles of constructive criticism. No one wants to walk that path, but everybody wants to reach that goal.

So, ask for feedback from people who know the craft. If you're running the sound mixer, ask people who have a good ear for music. If you're the worship leader, ask other worship leaders and the pastor. Then be willing to put their suggestions into practice as appropriate.

Grow spiritually, not just musically. I've said this before, and I will say it again: Grow spiritually, not just musically. Yes, you're not held to as strict a standard as those who teach God's Word. Yes, you're under the leadership of the church leaders or elders. But your role as a worship leader is so visible, your person so recognizable, and your responsibility so sacred that you must devote yourself to continually grow in the grace and knowledge of the Lord Jesus.

God will hold you accountable to grow spiritually, as should your congregation. You may know, deep down, that the congregation wouldn't dare hold you accountable because they need you. After all, you're the only one who knows how to play guitar or operate the sound system. But even if the humans around you don't hold you accountable, the Spirit will. So endeavor to continue to grow in the grace and knowledge of God, not just in your musical craft.

Beware that your musical gifts aren't so great that they seem to make up for your lack of spiritual qualifications. Pray that God in His mercy removes you from such a dangerous and destructive path. It may sound like I'm being overdramatic, but that's not the case. As a Christian leader, I care more for you and your relationship with God than how well you play music.

If I put your musical contribution above your walk with God, I'm not loving you. I'm just using you. Don't let others use you, and don't use yourself this way. Put your spiritual life before your musical life.

If you need to step back from up-front worship ministry so you can engage in pastoral counseling, do it. Yes, people will ask you why you're stepping down. "But you're so good at piano," they may say. "You have such a nice voice," they may say. But you must not neglect your spiritual walk.

What's the point of leading worship? To direct people to God.

If you step back from up-front leading for the sake of your walk, you're still modeling what it means to worship God with your whole life. You are leading yourself to worship God and others to worship Him because of your example.

Let the community of faith surround you as you pursue God afresh. And remember that you're not just a band member or a song leader, you're a worship leader.

Lead—and lead well.

WORKBOOK

Chapter Thirty-Nine Questions

Your Heart: Are you more committed to being "up front" or to leading worship through your life? When are times when the most spiritual thing a worship leader can do is to stop leading up-front to take care of their own walk with God first and foremost?

_____
_____
_____
_____
_____
_____
_____
_____
_____

Your Commitment: Work together as a team with your leaders to determine proper attire that will best honor God, serve the church's needs, and cause as little distraction as possible from your message. If helpful, plan out or write out general guidelines for clothing. (E.g., jeans or slacks? If skirts for women, what length? T-shirts or collared shirts?) Remember, the point is not to be legalistic, but to give guidance so that unnecessary attention will not be focused on appearance instead of worship.

_____

_____

_____

_____

_____

_____

_____

_____

_____

_____

Chapter Thirty-Nine Notes

CONCLUSION

It Starts with You

The ministry role of a worship leader is not an easy task. In addition to having your heart in the right place for sincere worship—and mentoring others to worship in spirit and in truth—there are countless practical aspects that go into being an excellent worship leader. Not to mention all the challenges you will encounter as you endeavor to lead worship with a high level of spiritual character and musical competency.

The outworking of your gift as a worship leader may look different depending on whether you serve a small or large congregation, or on the cultural, ethnic, and socioeconomic makeup of your church. However, all excellent worship leaders must become skilled at picking the best songs, arranging quality sets, and leading well.

Ultimately, leading your congregation to worship in reverence and awe is best done when you work hard to grow your skills, and lead by example as you foster reverence and awe for the Lord in your own heart and life.

REFERENCES

Notes

1. "Fast Facts about American Religion." Hartford Institute for Religion Research. 2000–2006. http://hirr.hartsem.edu/research/fastfacts/fast_facts.html#sizecong.

2. See Fig. 7.3 in Erin Meyer, *The Culture Map: Decoding How People Think, Lead, and Get Things Done Across Culture* (PublicAffairs, 2016).

3. Tarrant, Rick. "20: The Countdown Magazine Remembers Rich Mullins." Kidbrothers.net. October 11, 1997. http://kidbrothers.net/words/interviews/20-the-countdown-magazine-oct1197.html.

4. Townend, Stuart. "How Deep the Father's Love for Us." Kingsway's Thankyou Music, 1995.

5. Van Dyke, Henry J. "Joyful, Joyful, We Adore Thee." 1907. In Timeless Truths Free Online Library. https://library.timelesstruths.org/music/Joyful_Joyful_We_Adore_Thee.

6. Bancroft, Charitie Lees. "Before the Throne of God Above." 1863. In Hymnary.org. https://hymnary.org/text/before_the_throne_of_god_above_i_have_a_.

7. Myrin, Jonas, and Matt Redman. "You Alone Can Rescue." *We Shall Not Be Shaken*. Six Steps Records, 2010.
8. Schaeffer, Francis A. *Art and the Bible*. IVP Books, 2009.
9. Associated Press. "Baseball Great Ted Williams Dies at 83. *New York Times*. July 5, 2002. https://www.nytimes.com/2002/07/05/sports/baseball-great-ted-williams-dies-at-83.html.
10. Altrogge, Mark. "I Stand in Awe." Sovereign Grace Praise, 1987. In Hymnary.org. https://hymnary.org/text/you_are_beautiful_beyond_description.
11. Hillsong. "Forever." Lyrics by Marty Sampson. *You Are My World*. Hillsong Music Australia, 2001.
12. Heber, Reginald. "Holy, Holy, Holy! Lord God Almighty!" 1826. In Hymnary.org. https://hymnary.org/text/holy_holy_holy_lord_god_almighty_early.
13. Smith, Martin. "I Could Sing of Your Love Forever." Mercy Vineyard, 1996. In E-Chords.com. https://www.e-chords.com/chords/martin-smith/i-could-sing-of-your-love-forever.
14. Tomlin, Chris. "Made to Worship." Lyrics by John P. Kee. *See the Morning*. Sparrow Records, 2006.
15. Chris Tomlin. "How Great Is Our God." Lyrics by Chris Tomlin, Ed Cash, and Jesse Reeves. *Arriving*. Sparrow Records, 2004.

APPENDIX A

Song Categorizing Worksheet

1. What is the song's message?
    A. Is the message biblical and God-exalting?
    B. What is the mood or theme of the song?
2. What is the song's music?
    A. Is the music well written? Do the lyrics match well with the music?
3. Does the song match the context?
    A. Can my team play the song well enough for the occasion and our congregation?
    B. How well does the song match our congregation's musical tastes and abilities?
4. How is God exalted by the song?
    A. Is God the subject or object of the song?
5. Fact or Feeling?
    A. Is this song stating facts about God, our relationship to Him, etc.?

B. Or is it a song that expresses feeling or opinions?
6. Is the song a focusing song or an expressing song?

APPENDIX B

Set Assessment Checklist

1. Do my songs fit thematically?
2. Do I know the movements of multiple songs in my overall set?
3. Will my congregation be ready to respond by the time we get to songs of sentiments and feelings?
4. Does my set progress from God as subject to God as object?
5. Does my set rehearse the gospel?
6. Am I balancing the songs, mood, and content within this single set?
7. Am I balancing the songs, theology, and styles over multiple sets in my congregation?
8. Will this set end strong, that is, with a bang?

APPENDIX C

Samples of "Call to Worship"

The following pages contain samples of how Scripture can be used for congregation worship and responsive reading. The principles used to format these are found in Chapter Twenty-Two, entitled "Worship with Scripture."

Call to Worship:
From 1 Chronicles 29:10–13 (NIV)

Leader: Praise be to you, O LORD,
    God of our father Israel,
    From everlasting to everlasting.

All: Yours, O LORD, is the greatness and the power
    And the glory and the majesty and the splendor,
    For everything in heaven and earth is yours.

Leader: Yours, O LORD, is the kingdom;
    You are exalted as head over all.

All: Wealth and honor come from you;
    You are the ruler of all things.

Leader: In Your hands are strength and power to exalt
    And give strength to all.

All: Now, our God, we give you thanks
    and praise Your glorious name.

Call to Worship:
From Psalm 31:1–5 (NIV)

Leader: In you, O LORD, I have taken refuge;
Let me never be put to shame;
Deliver me in your righteousness.

All: Be my rock of refuge,
A strong fortress to save me.

Leader: Since you are my rock and my fortress,
For the sake of your name lead and guide me.

All: Into your hands I commit my spirit
Deliver me, LORD, my faithful God.

Call to Worship:
From Psalm 47 (NIV)

Leader: God has ascended amid shouts of joy,
the LORD amid the sounding of trumpets.

All: Sing praises to God, sing praises;
sing praises to our King, sing praises.

Leader: For God is the King of all the earth;
sing to him a psalm of praise.

All: God reigns over the nations;
God is seated on his holy throne.

Leader: Clap your hands, all you nations;
shout to God with cries of joy.

All: How awesome is the LORD Most High,
the great King over all the earth!

Call to Worship:
From Psalm 67 (NIV)

Leader: May God be gracious to us and bless us
And make his face shine upon us.

All: May the peoples praise You, O God.
May all the peoples praise you.

Leader: May the nations be glad and sing for joy,
For You rule the peoples justly

All: May the peoples praise You, O God.
May all the peoples praise You.

Leader: Then the land will yield its harvest,
And God, our God, will bless us.

All: God will bless us,
And all the ends of the earth will fear him.

Call to Worship:
From Psalm 73 (NIV)

Leader: Whom have I in heaven but you?
    And earth has nothing I desire besides you.

All: My flesh and my heart may fail,
    But God is the strength of my heart
    And my portion forever.

Leader: Those who are far from you will perish;
    You destroy all who are unfaithful to you.

All: But as for me, it is good to be near God.
    I have made the Sovereign LORD my refuge;
    I will tell of all your deeds.

Call to Worship:
From Psalm 146 (NASB)

Leader: Praise the LORD!
　　　　Praise the LORD, O my soul!

All: I will praise the LORD while I live.
　　I will sing praises to my God while
　　I have my being.

Leader: Do not trust in princes,
　　　　In mortal man, in whom there is no salvation.

All: How blessed is he whose help is the God of Jacob,
　　Whose hope is in the LORD his God,
　　Who made heaven and earth,
　　The sea and all that is in them;
　　Who keeps faith forever.

Call to Worship:
From Isaiah 53 (NIV)

Leader: Who has believed our message
  and to whom has the arm of the LORD been revealed?

All: He grew up before him like a tender shoot,
  And like a root out of dry ground.

Leader: He had no beauty or majesty to attract us to him,
  Nothing in his appearance that we should
  desire him.

All: He was despised and rejected by men,
  A man of sorrows, and familiar with suffering.

Leader: Surely he took up our infirmities
  And carried our sorrows,
  Yet we considered him stricken by God,
  Smitten by him, and afflicted.

All: But he was pierced for our transgressions,
  He was crushed for our iniquities;
  The punishment that brought us peace was upon him,
  And by his wounds we are healed.

All: We all, like sheep, have gone astray,
  Each of us has turned to his own way;
  And the LORD has laid on him
  The iniquity of us all.

Call to Worship:
From 1 Corinthians 15 (NIV)

Leader: Now, brothers, I want to remind you
of the gospel I preached to you,
which you received and on which
you have taken your stand.

All: By this gospel we are saved,
if only we hold firmly
to the word preached to us.
Otherwise, we have believed in vain.

Leader: For what I received I passed on to you
as of first importance:

All: That Christ died for our sins according
to the Scriptures, that he was buried,
that he was raised on the third day
according to the Scriptures,
and that he appeared to Peter,
and then to the Twelve.

Leader: But Christ has been raised from
the dead, the first-fruits of those who
have fallen asleep.

All: For since death came through a man,
the resurrection of the dead comes also
through a man.
For as in Adam all die,
so in Christ all will be made alive.

Leader: "Where, O death, is your victory?
Where, O death, is your sting?"

*All: The sting of death is sin,
and the power of sin is the law.
But thanks be to God!
He gives us the victory through our Lord Jesus Christ.*

Call to Worship:
From Philippians 3 (NIV)

Leader: But whatever was to my profit
I now consider loss for the sake of Christ.

*All: What is more, I consider everything a loss compared
to the surpassing greatness of knowing
Christ Jesus my Lord,
for whose sake I have lost all things.*

Leader: I consider them rubbish, that I may gain Christ
And be found in him.

*All: Not having a righteousness of my own that comes
from the law,
But that which is through faith in Christ.*

Leader: The righteousness that comes from God
and is by faith.

*All: I want to know Christ
and the power of his resurrection
And the fellowship of sharing in his sufferings,
Becoming like him in his death,
And so, somehow, to attain to the resurrection
from the dead.*

Call to Worship:
From 1 Peter 1 (NIV)

Leader: Therefore, prepare your minds for action;
Be self-controlled.

All: Set your hope fully on the grace to be given you
When Jesus Christ is revealed.

Leader: As obedient children, do not conform to the evil desires you had when you lived in ignorance.

All: But just as he who called you is holy,
so be holy in all you do;
For it is written, "Be holy, because I am holy."

About the Author

Enoch Liao has served in pastoral and worship ministries for over twenty years. He currently serves at Boston Chinese Evangelical Church in both their inner city and suburban campuses. He is married to Karen, and they have three sons at home and one daughter who has passed on. Enoch received his education from UCLA and Talbot School of Theology in California, where both he and Karen grew up. They live in Medford, MA.

www.ingramcontent.com/pod-product-compliance
Lightning Source LLC
Chambersburg PA
CBHW070135100426
42743CB00013B/2709